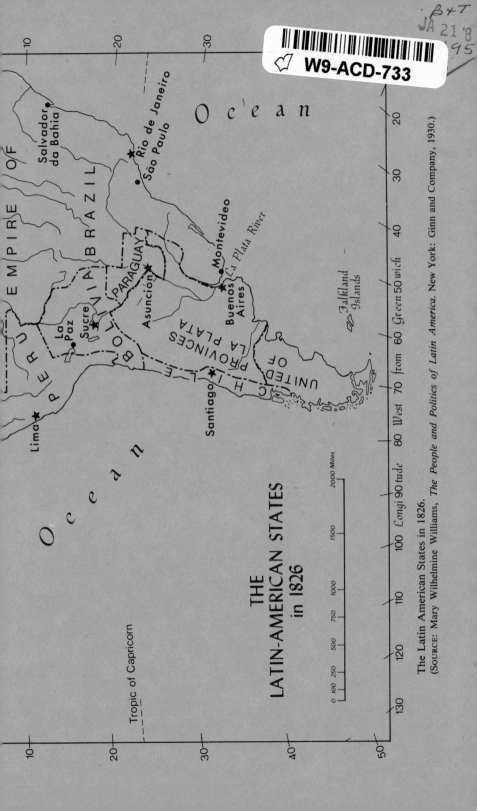

THE
LATIN-AMERICAN STATES
in 1826

The Latin American States in 1826.
(SOURCE: Mary Wilhelmine Williams, *The People and Politics of Latin America*. New York: Ginn and Company, 1930.)

THE POVERTY OF PROGRESS

THE POVERTY OF PROGRESS

Latin America in the Nineteenth Century

E. Bradford Burns

UNIVERSITY OF CALIFORNIA PRESS
Berkeley   Los Angeles   London

University of California Press
Berkeley and Los Angeles, California

University of California Press, Ltd.
London, England

Library of Congress Cataloging in Publication Data

Burns, E Bradford.
    The poverty of progress.

    Includes index.
    1. Latin America—History—1830-1898.
2. Latin America—Social conditions. 3. Latin
America—Economic conditions. I. Title.
F1413.B87   980'.03   80-51236
ISBN 0-520-04160-7

Printed in the United States of America

"Peoples of Europe, if only the sea and wind had never brought you to us! Ah, it was not for nothing that nature extended between us that flat expanse of waters."

—Words of the Indian Cacambo, Basílio de Gama, *O Uraguai*

"The incorporation of America into 'Western Civilization' was marked by violence first against the Indian population and later against the black slaves and the mestizo population."

—Alvaro Tirado Mejía,
Aspectos Sociales de las Guerras Civiles en Colombia

"And at last the philosophy of progress shows its true face: a featureless blank. We know now that the kingdom of progress is not of this world: the paradise it promises us is in the future, a future that is impalpable, unreachable, perpetual. Progress has peopled history with the marvels and monsters of technology but it has depopulated the life of man. It has given us more things but not more being. . . . How can we not turn away and seek another mode of development? It is an urgent task that requires both science and imagination, both honesty and sensitivity; a task without precedence, because all of the modes of development that we know, whether they come from the West or the East, lead to disaster. Under the present circumstances the race toward development is mere haste to reach ruin."

—Octavio Paz, *The Other Mexico: Critique of the Pyramid*

One of the reasons I had wanted to go back to a traditional peasant society was to see if, as Fromm and Maccoby had suggested, there was a higher level of productiveness and a greater enjoyment of life than in the mestizo village which they had studied and with which I was also quite familiar. Again, as I have repeatedly observed, there does in fact appear to be a greater enjoyment of life among the Chan Kom women than there had been observed in Las Cuevas, or in most mestizo villages, or for that matter, in most communities in the U.S.A. The women constantly display their sense of pride and pleasure in most aspects of their lives, conveying a feeling of dignity as well as pride. And, more importantly, there is a sense of harmony with each other, with nature, within their total world."

—Mary Lindsay Elendorf,
Nine Mayan Women: A Village Faces Change

"The quality of human existence is the ultimate measure of development."

—Alan Berg,
The Nutrition Factor: Its Role in National Development

CONTENTS

PREFACE

If this essay succeeds, it will open an interpretive window providing a different perspective of Latin America's recent past. At first glance, the view might seem to be of the conventional landscape of modernization, but I hope a steady gaze will reveal it to be far vaster and more complex. For one thing, rather than enumerating the benefits accruing to Latin America as modernization became a dominant feature of the social, economic, and political life of the region, this essay regards the imposition of modernization as the catalyst of a devastating cultural struggle and as a barrier to Latin America's development. Clearly if a window to the past is opened by this essay, then so too is a new door to controversy.

After most of the nations of Latin America gained political independence, their leaders rapidly accelerated trends more leisurely under way since the closing decades of the eighteenth century: the importation of technology and ideas with their accompanying values from Western Europe north of the Pyrenees and the full entrance into the world's capitalistic marketplace. Such trends shaped those new nations more profoundly than their advocates probably had realized possible. Their promoters moved forward steadfastly within the legacy of some basic institutions bequeathed by centuries of Iberian rule. That combination of hoary institutions with newer, non-Iberian technology, values, and ideas forged contemporary Latin America with its enigma of overwhelming poverty amid potential plenty.

This essay emphasizes that the victory of the European-oriented ruling elites over the Latin American folk with their community values resulted only after a long and violent struggle, which characterized most of the nineteenth century. Whatever advantages might have resulted from the success of the elites, the victory also fastened two dominant and interrelated characteristics on contemporary Latin America: a deepening dependency and the declining quality of life for the majority.

We know little of the struggles of the folk and weakly appreciate their motivations. Apparently the less European-oriented peoples were determined to safeguard their own cultural past with which they were not only familiar but from which they felt they derived greater benefits. Obviously we should know more of their attitudes, rationale, ways of life, and alternatives to rapid modernization and to capitalism in order to better understand Latin America's historical process. The folk were wary of modernization, at least in the forms it took in the nineteenth century. Apparently they had good reasons to be. Their quality of life declined as modernization accelerated. The contrasting and conflicting goals of the elites and the folk provide a dramatic dialectic. I suggest it might constitute the essence of nineteenth-century Latin American history.

This speculative essay asks the reader to consider revising some standard views of nineteenth-century Latin America and to consider the possibility that folk societies and cultures derived from Ibero-Afro-Indian experiences might have provided life-style alternatives more advantageous to the masses than the Europeanized modernization imposed on them. In doing so, it is intentionally polemical. It consciously questions some widely accepted concepts, theses, and interpretations, partly to urge they be reconsidered, partly to broaden them. Some perhaps should be replaced. My hope is that this essay will stimulate further discussion in an effort to reassess the nineteenth century, a key period in Latin American history, an understanding of which is requisite for any meaningful analysis of contemporary Latin America.

Admittedly the essay sweeps broadly across vast geographical and temporal spaces. It is at best suggestive. More research and evidence will be necessary to sustain these theses. Let us regard the essay, then, as the possible beginning of a reinterpretation. However, the essay claims originality only on the basis of its broad sweep. Otherwise, it has brought together some ideas suggested and evidence documented by an historical revisionism already under way in Latin America, Europe, and the United States. I owe much to those scholars whose monographic studies have provided novel glimpses into the last century as well as valuable data. In the notes following the text, I pay tribute to many of those pioneering works and to their authors. Naturally I assume responsibility for the theses in this essay and, indeed, for the interpretations I place on statistics and data drawn from others.

E. Bradford Burns

Hollywood Hills
February 1980

Popular Governments of Latin America

The period between 1849 and 1852 marked the high point of popular governments in nineteenth-century Latin America. Folk leaders or caudillos dominated Argentina, Paraguay, Bolivia, Guatemala, and Yucatan.

CHAPTER ONE

The Nineteenth Century:
Progress and Cultural Conflict

Cultural conflict characterized nineteenth-century Latin America. On the one hand, the elites, increasingly enamored with the modernization first of an industrializing Europe and then of the United States, insisted on importing and imposing those foreign patterns on their fledgling nations. They became increasingly convinced that Europe and the United States offered solutions to the problems they perceived in their societies as well as a life-style to their liking. On the other hand, the vast majority of Latin Americans, other elites but most particularly the popular classes, recognized the threat inherent in the wholesale importation of modernization and the capitalism accompanying it. They resisted, preferring their long-established living patterns to the more recent foreign novelties and fearful of their impact on their lives. The conflict between the two groups intensified as the century matured. In the struggle the Europeanized elites did not hesitate to repress their more numerous opposition who clung to their preferences and when necessary used physical means in an effort to preserve them.

No single elite espousing a uniform doctrine ever existed. Despite their variety, however, they shared a general outlook and they took actions that increasingly in the nineteenth century harmed the folk. That plurality of elites, because of their skills, contacts, powers, adaptability, intelligence, birth, and/or wealth, exercised an unusual degree of authority. They controlled the governmental institutions, as well as the commerce, banking, agriculture, and arts. They tended to make or to influence the making of significant economic and political decisions in their regions or nations. Likewise, the folk manifested a heterogeneity that challenges generalization in so vast an area as Latin America. And yet, as in the case of the elites, the folk, when all was said and done, manifested certain broad tendencies of behavior that gave them generally recognizable and somewhat similar characteristics as we shall later see.

While cultural clash was not unique to nineteenth-century Latin America, the intensity seldom had been equalled before and has not been approached since. To some degree it had characterized this hemisphere for thousands of years as Indian empires expanded, encroached on other Indian groups, and imposed new cultures. In the sixteenth century, the clash assumed different and more complex forms, first with the Iberian invasion and conquest and then with the importation of slaves from Africa. The cultural clash that we know most about pitted Indian civilizations against Iberian. Indian rebellions against European rule and cultural imposition frequently erupted during the long colonial period. As mestizo and mulatto cultures took shape, borrowing as they did from the Indo-Afro-European experiences, as the number of slaves and manumitted blacks rose as well as the number of settlements of runaway slaves, as the immigration of Iberian peasants into Latin America expanded, the variation and complexity of cultural expressions and the possibility of symbiosis or of conflict also increased. In at least one aspect, the nineteenth century was unique: it was the last opportunity for those most identified with the New World, the folk societies and their cultures, to exert influence over local, regional, or even national life. However, by the final decades of the century and certainly by the first of the twentieth century, those once vigorous folk societies had lost the struggle. They no longer were viable alternatives to the Europeanization that was taking place on an unprecedented scale.

The period in this essay denoted the nineteenth century defies precise definition. At best its boundaries blur. This temporal term encompasses those years after the new nations declared and won their political independence. (Symbolically we could use the date 1821, realizing that Haiti was independent by 1804 and that Brazil did not exert its independence until 1822, while the Spanish-speaking nations broke their relationship with Madrid at a variety of times from 1810 to 1822.) For purposes of this essay, then, the nineteenth century began when the new nations of Latin America assumed responsibility for their political destinies. This period ended sometime during the second decade of the twentieth century, terminated by the outbreak of a major revolution in Mexico whose potential for the creation of an autochthonous society seemed to mark a significant break with the past, by World War I, which disturbed established export and dependency patterns forcing a new relationship between Latin America and its nineteenth-century mentors England and France, and by the rise to power of the United States with the further spread of its influence throughout all of Latin America. It was all too evident by that time that the drive toward increasing urbanization, industrialization, and modernization had accelerated; while at the same time, and contradictory to that drive only on the most superficial level, the latifundio, export economies, and dependency characterized life in these new countries of the Western Hemisphere. The governments of the elites had selected the North Atlantic model for their countries to follow and forced the opposition to bend to that decision.

The nations of the North Atlantic during the nineteenth century spawned a remarkable technology, which in turn facilitated their development. Infrastructures of roads, canals, and railroads solidified national unity while encouraging commerce and industry. Steamships and/or railroads circulated commerce, ideas, and peoples among those nations more readily and swiftly. Industrialization and urbanization, reshaping the economies as well as the demographies, required increasing amounts of agrarian products and raw materials. The population surge unleashed by medical advances further added to those requirements. Rapid accumulation of capital prompted investors to look abroad for lucrative investments, and Latin America with its natural resources and vast potential beckoned. There, the North Atlantic capitalists invested, sold their manufactured surpluses, and purchased national or agrarian products. By 1914, they had invested $8.5 billion in Latin America. The British put fully twenty percent of their overseas investment there. Generally most of the Latin American elites welcomed those investments and accepted their attendant consequences. They respected the cultures that made possible such capital accumulation, awesome technology, and pleasant lifestyles.

Influenced by the political and economic ideas of the Enlightenment at the time of their political independence, the ruling elites imposed upon Latin America theories that reflected little or none of the local socioeconomic environment. The precise political labels adopted by the elites varied, although they tended to group themselves under the headings of Liberals and Conservatives. Those labels confused rather than clarified because the elites had much more in common than in opposition. They tended to gravitate toward what was considered in the broadest terms of the Enlightenment to be liberal for the early nineteenth century: a written constitution that circumscribed the chief executive who shared power at least nominally with a legislature and judiciary; a limitation, if not outright abolition, of restrictions on trade; public education; and formal equality before the law. Liberty and democracy as the dominant elites perceived and pursued them throughout most of the nineteenth century in a majority of the Latin American nations sanctioned individualism, competition, and the unfettered pursuit of profit. They tended to be abstract, exclusive, and dependent on authority. In the classical sense, liberalism meant placing individual freedom and material gain over public interest. The elites felt they shaped their institutions in the latest European molds. They ignored the obvious fact that those models did not reflect American experience. As one immediate consequence the European models sired weak and compliant economic structures in the New World. They also favored the strong, wealthy, and resourceful minority over the huge, but weakened majority.

The elites spoke constantly of "progress," perhaps the most sacred word in the political vocabulary but also one with an awesome array of meanings. Later generations of scholars substituted the word *modernization,* but that replacement did little to clarify the concept. Both words, used interchangeably hereafter, implied an admiration for the latest ideas, modes, values, inventions, and styles of Europe and the United States and a desire to adopt—rarely to adapt—them. The elites believed that "to progress" meant to recreate their nations as closely as possible to their European and North American models. They felt they would benefit from such a recreation, and by extension they assumed that their nations would benefit as well. They always identified (and confused) class well-being with national welfare.

The economic system that the elites obviously associated with progress was capitalism. It could not be otherwise when their primary models were England, France, and the United States. True, in large parts of Latin America long before independence, a type of neocapitalism already had penetrated and under Iberian institutions had influenced Latin American societies. It shaped at least a part of local customs as they evolved over the centuries. A high degree of mediation of values existed in those distant realms of the multicultural Iberian empires. European ideas and techniques filtered slowly, selectively through local customs, a process more notable outside the major cities and ports of course. But symbiosis characterized the cultures even in those urban areas. To a greater or lesser degree, depending on the area, the Iberian authorities had worked out with the inhabitants of their New World empires a modus operandi that respected or tolerated many local customs. If the local populations converted nominally to Roman Catholicism, acknowledged the supremacy of Iberian monarchs, and supplied labor when needed by the Europeans, they were left largely alone. Also, they received a kind of protection from crown and church as well as a certain minimal security from the local neofeudalistic landowners. In short, a type of compromise had been reached between Iberian demands and local customs. Like most compromises it suited neither side perfectly, but both accepted it as preferable to other alternatives. At any rate, the penetration of that Iberian neocapitalism was incomplete and by no means as challenging to the local populations and their cultures after the initial conquest period as was North Atlantic capitalism after 1821, particularly after midcentury.

As it turned out, old Iberian policies facilitated the adoption by the new Latin American governments of the neoclassical economic model imposed by the Northern Europeans.

Latin America was to trade those items it produced cheaply (agrarian and mineral products) for those items it did not produce or could not do so cheaply (manufactured goods). Such a trade patern derived from the complementary division of labor was supposed to benefit all. Only the passage of time revealed to the Latin Americans the mischief masked by facile theory.

The constitution, laws, and political practices the ruling elites put into effect complemented the penetration and growth of capitalism in Latin America. In nineteenth-century practice, the landlords produced their sugarcane, wool, beef, wheat, coffee, indigo, cacao, or other crops on as large a scale as possible for sale in an external market from which they expected a satisfactory profit. The politicians approved foreign exploitation of the natural resources with the hope that some residue of the wealth created would enrich them and facilitate the transformation of at least the capital cities into citadels of European culture. The wealth created from the countryside and mines, shared increasingly with middlemen in the ports, brought landlords and politicians prestige, and the combination of wealth and prestige conferred power. The growing merchant class dependent on the one hand on the flow of primary products from the countryside to the exterior and on the other on the ability of the landed gentry and bureaucrats to afford costly European imports exhibited scant inclination to challenge a system that also benefited them. Certainly differences separted them, but at the same time it was not uncommon that obvious benefits to be derived from the political, economic, and social systems encouraged an unarticulated alliance between the bureaucrats, politicians, merchants, and landlords who dominated the new nations, an alliance strengthened by pervasive and intricate kinship patterns.

In the course of the nineteenth century, Latin America acquired many of the accoutrements of progress: railroads, steamships, electricity, machinery, Parisian fashions, and English textiles. Many a city displayed a European "facade." Guatemala City boasted that it was the "Paris of Central America," while Buenos Aires claimed to be the "Paris of South America," titles hotly disputed by other Latin American metropolises. But while progress might have materially improved the lot of some elites, whetted the appetites of the emerging middle classes, and won the approval of the European mentors, it plunged Latin America into deeper dependency. Its cost emptied local treasuries. What should be more alarming, however, it impoverished the majority of the Latin Americans, who were no better off at the end of the century than they had been at the beginning. In fact, the argument can be put forth that they were worse off.

Profoundly altering the concepts of land and labor, North Atlantic capitalism clashed with the practices and ideology of the Latin American folk. The individual rights almost universally promised by the idealistic, if unrealistic constitutions proved meaningless to a repressed majority. In fact, the values the elites placed on abstract liberties and democracy conflicted with the values and experiences of the largest numbers of the population, who understood little of European theories and nothing of the European experience that gave rise to them. With experiences rooted in the New World, they drew from a past of interdependence, cooperation, solidarity, and a harmony contrary to the theories of individuality and competition. Not prepared for the values imposed by the elites, the masses could not hope to gain much from them. In fact, they did not. Liberty and democracy as they took form in nineteenth-century Latin America quickly became a sophistic rationale excusing or disguising an exploitation of the many by the few. As one Argentine historian, Hector Iñigo Carrera, expressed it, "Liberalism promised a theoretical garden of happiness which historically became a jungle of poverty."

The masses often repudiated the values imposed on them and attempted to express their own. That expression more often than not falls under the classification of "folklore," to which a certain pejorative sense or condescension often is attached by scholars. One function that folk culture assumes before the "official" cultures is protest, whether consciously or not. Folk values readily reveal the limitations of the universality of the "official" values. Throughout Latin America a viable popular culture existed—and still does—which either challenged official culture or adapted to it or evolved parallel, albeit subordinate, to it.

The lands the folk once worked, often lands that served entire communities and constituted a fundamental factor in personal, environmental, and ecological relationships, became a commodity to be bought and sold under rapidly expanding capitalism. Lands that had succeeded in remaining outside of or peripheral to Iberian neocapitalism passed from community or peasant control into the hands of fewer and fewer owners who often withheld them from use as an investment or as one means of dominating scarce labor supply or cultivated them to produce items that had little or no local use but sold profitably in distant markets. By the end of the century, the folk had lost control of most of the lands they once had worked. Further, they were forced to sell their labor to the hacienda and plantation owners for a minimal return, and in that arrangement some of them were employed only a few months of each year. Absorption of Indian lands by the Iberians and forced labor imposed by those Iberians and their New World descendants had characterized the colonial period, but the nineteenth century witnessed a faster pace of absorption of land, a tougher exploitation of labor, and stronger pressures on the folk to abandon local ways for those that seemed more European or more attuned to the ways of capitalism. Those trends accelerated with each passing decade. At the same time as land was concentrated in fewer hands, the population of Latin America rose rapidly, doubling from approximately 30.5 million in 1850 to 61 million by 1900. The problems caused by an expanding population and restricted land owning can be readily understood. Besides the obvious rural problems, acute urban ones burgeoned when the desperate rural masses increasingly sought relief in cities totally unprepared to receive them.

Since the labor of those folk and their relationship to the land had constituted well-established patterns of behavior, the rapid and extensive change to commercial agriculture and the accelerated emphasis on an export economy traumatized their lives. Relentlessly challenged by the export sector, the folk societies disintegrated. Each phase of modernization seemed to increase the pressure. Local communities became a part of a larger, more distant, more impersonal, and more pervasive economic system to which the folk sacrificed their land, labor, and life styles but from which they received scant or no benefits. Those changes to suit the rising demands of distant metropolises surpassed the realm of economics to challenge cultural values. The ensuing cultural conflicts, brutal, prolonged, and universal (in the sense that they characterized almost every

region of Latin America) with the eventual triumph of Europeanization, emerge as an interpretive theme giving significance and meaning to nineteenth-century Latin American
history and shaping the twentieth century.

This interpretation neither invalidates nor supersedes other
approaches to the study of the nineteenth century. Rather, it
tries to add some depth and a greater understanding to customary treatments of the past.

Older histories of the century after
independence dwelt on the apparent chaos, the rapidly changing governments in Mexico, Honduras, Nicaragua, Colombia,
Venezuela, Ecuador, Peru, Bolivia, Urugray, and at certain
times Argentina; the short-lived constitutions (the Latin
Americans have written 180 to 190 of them, a large percentage
of which were adopted and abandoned before 1850); and political struggles that erupted into bloody civil wars between conservatives and liberals in Mexico, Central America, Colombia,
Bolivia, and Chile. Many historical treatments of the nineteenth century seem to collapse into a welter of governments
and resort to bewildering lists of presidents with accompanying
comments on the "good" and "bad" they might have done.
Later, builiding on factual accumulations, historians gave emphasis first to the consolidation of independence and the search
for political stability and then to the pursuit of economic prosperity, which seemed to provide handy compartments in which
to fit the first and then the second halves of the century,
although most of the varied nations resisted such neat pack-
aging. The second half of the nineteenth century, which witnessed some economic growth and fitful periods of prosperity
for the elites, became associated with urbanization, industrialization, and modernization. The latter began to assume importance as a useful interpretive theme. Carefully constructed
definitions were assigned (sometimes) to the illusive term
modernization, but despite the search for deep meaning the
drive to modernize in nineteenth-century Latin America usually and simply meant an eagerness on the part of the governing elites to ape Europe. Whether the term *modernization* (or
its nineteenth-century equivalent, *progress*) was used or not,
most historical judgments of Latin America, whether by local
or foreign historians, were made on the basis of the degree of
modernization, progress, or Europeanization visible. Historians

applauded the long stability of Chile and Brazil in the nineteenth century and attributed their early and apparent, if cosmetic, modernization to that good order. Likewise they observed that progress characterized Argentina and Mexico only after order superseded chaos in the last half of the century. Certainly the forms modernization assumed introduced new opportunities and benefits for some Latin Americans. The more enthusiastic historians have written about economic development in the nineteenth century, while the more cautious have conceded growth. It would be a rare historian who did not conclude that Latin America was better off at the end of the century that at the beginning.

By focusing attention now on cultural conflict during the nineteenth century, this essay raises some questions about the efficacy — and certainly about the desirability — of modernization or progress. From the point of view of the majority, did rapid modernization create problems or opportunities? If, indeed, modernization was desirable and beneficial, then why did so many people oppose it so violently? Were those opponents simply perverse or ignorant or ungrateful? Do the claims that modernization benefited Latin America extend to all or at least to a majority of the Latin Americans? These questions deserve consideration, and this essay is intended to suggest some tentative answers.

A study of cultural conflict in the past century can provide some useful insights and perhaps serve as one guide to interpret that complex period of Latin American history. It should remind us that resistance to modernization was much more intense and widespread than official historiography would have us believe, while at the same time offering an understanding of folk opposition to the elites' plans. Further, it helps to explain some of the major problems besetting contemporary Latin America, in particular those revolving around questions of dependency and development. Like all generalities sweeping across vast geographical and temporal spaces it contains weaknesses as well as strengths. For one thing, we know far more about elite preferences than popular ones, and hence we tend to see the elitist view of the past with greater precision and will continue to do so until more research better clarifies the alternatives. For another, it is difficult to generalize about the diverse peoples and myriad events that compose a century of the history of such a varied area as Latin America. Lumped together in generalities are the national experiences of such a territorial giant as Brazil with its three and a quarter million square miles and tiny El Salvador with its eight thousand square miles; of countries of great natural resources and tremendous potential with those of very limited means of support for their inhabitants; of nations with large black populations: Brazil, Haiti, the Dominican Republic, and Venezuela; large Indian populations: Mexico, Guatemala, Ecuador, Peru, Bolivia, and Paraguay; and large European populations: Argentina, Uruguay, and Chile; and these are only some of the obvious differences. Nonetheless, this broad interpretation is possible because varied as those eighteen nations might have been, they also shared some very basic experiences with each other: political independence from Europe at approximately the same time and for many of the same reasons; inherited institutions and socio-economic structures—the latifundio, for example—which were similar; identical ideological influences from England and France and to a lesser degree from the United States; populations divided into a huge impoverished class on the one hand and the minute middle and upper classes that enjoyed nearly all the privileges, wealth, and power on the other; a driving desire on the part of many within those privileged classes to remake their nations according to patterns drawn first from England and France and later from the United States; and the presence of folk societies and folk cultures, varied as they might have been, which resisted rapid Europeanization.

The first temptation raised by this interpretation is to see the cultural conflict in terms of class struggle. Unquestionably class struggles existed. But that oversimplification should be avoided in homage to the richness and complexity of the myriad events of nineteenth-century Latin America. True, those favoring the shaping of Latin America in the European-United States image with the attendant modernization and imposition of capitalism generally speaking were associated with the upper classes, the socioeconomic and political elites. After all, they enjoyed the most ready access to Western ideas and seemed best situated to benefit from Westernization. However, it is equally true that large numbers of the elites also hesitated to embrace the ideas and ways of Northern Europe and the United States, clinging to the Iberian past and the American experience. The interests of the traditional rural patriarchs did not always harmonize with those of the landowners eager to modernize their estates in order to take advantage of export markets and of the merchants, bureaucrats, and other members of the affluent urban bourgeoisie. Whereas the economic inclinations of both the patriarchs and other groups might have dictated continued, if not intensified, exportation of agrarian and mineral items, their cultural preferences separated them. The former maintained a greater loyalty to the past, while the latter sighed for a Europeanized future. Although the masses swayed often to favor various positions, most of them evinced a loyalty to the life-styles associated with folk societies or cultures, terms and concepts on which this essay expands later. Thus, at least three groups interacted around questions of modernization. Part of the elites and most of the middle class desired to reshape Latin America in the image of Northern Europe. The patriarchs, the Roman Catholic Church, and some intellectuals questioned rapid and unselective modernization and looked more to the Ibero-American past for guidance. Finally, the common people drew heavily on their own rich folk cultures — with which certain intellectuals sympathized — which to their thinking provided a satisfactory life-style they were reluctant to abandon. The positions taken toward modernization did not strictly follow class lines and for that reason confound the class struggle approach to this theme. Yet a struggle there was and, if not along clearly delineated class lines, then surely among cultural preferences.

In an attempt to provide an interpretive thesis for nineteenth-century Latin American history in the pages that follow, this essay will focus first on the faith exalted by the elites and middle class in modernization or progress; then consider the reservations of other members of the same elites as well as their alternatives before moving to the more difficult problem of determining the desires of the greater numbers of the humbler classes, by far the majority, in Latin America. In most cases rapid modernization threatened the more static folk societies and cultures and further accentuated the economic injustices prevalent in Latin America. As the thrust to modernize intensified, a clash between the modernizers and the folk became inevitable. Violence emerged as a letimotif of the nineteenth century, emphasizing a relationship between the lack of social and economic justice and social protest.

CHAPTER TWO

The Elite Preference for Progress

The Latin American elites of the nineteenth century boasted of their European heritage and even those with Indian and/or African ancestors dwelt more on their European ties than otherwise. England and France, in particular, were their models enhanced by distance, some misconceptions, and the elites' fears of their own provinciality or inferiority. They readily understood what was happening in Europe and ably discussed the latest ideas radiating from the Old World, which they welcomed to the New. But European thought was no intellectual spring; it proved to be an ideological flood, which swept before it most American originality. Generally speaking, three major European philosophies shaped the ideology of the elites during the nineteenth century: the Enlightenment, the ideas of evolution put forth by Charles Darwin and Herbert Spencer, and Positivism. The concept of "progress," perhaps the key word for the understanding of nineteenth-century Latin American history, linked the three.

Stressing the vincibility of ignorance, the Enlightenment philosophers concluded that if people had the opportunity to know the truth, they would select "civilization" over "barbarism." Adherents to the Enlightenment believed in a universally valid standard to judge "civilization," and the criteria for such a judgment rested on European concepts of progress. Civilization and the progress that led to it became identified with Europe, or more specifically with England, France, and Germany. Moreover, a burgeoning faith in science directed judgments on progress itself away from philosophical and moral matters toward material change. The popularized idea of Darwin that organic forms developed over the course of time and represented successive states in a single evolutionary process toward perfection further heightened the interest in progress, giving it a scientific veneer. Very propitiously, Spencer, who enjoyed tremendous circulation in nineteenth-century Latin America, applied the same principle of evolution to society. To Spencer progress signified a march toward "the establishment of the greatest perfection and the most complete happiness." However, that march subsumed a great many economic changes and adaptations. As one example, Spencer advocated railroads as a vital part of the organic system of a modern society. As another, he regarded industrialization as a certain manifestation of progress. Many Latin Americans drew from Spencer the interrelationship of science, industry, and progress, a combination pointing to future glory through societal evolution. Like most European thinkers, Spencer said much that damned Latin America; his racism, for example. The Latin Americans proved to be selective readers, however, choosing to ignore what displeased — or frightened — them.

Many of the ideas on progress pulled from the Enlightenment, Darwin, Spencer, as well as other sources, seemed to converge in the form Auguste Comte's Positivism assumed in Latin America during the last decades of the century. To Comte that progress was attainable through the acceptance of scientific laws codified by Positivism. Outward manifestations of progress — again railroads and industrialization — assumed great importance in positivism and emphatically so among the Latin Americans, whether they acknowledged Comte or not.

A part of the elites had initiated a serious and escalating questioning of some of the Iberian values during the last decades of the eighteenth century. It goes without saying that they were even more critical of Indian and African contributions to Latin American life if, in fact, they ever considered them. Increased contacts with Northern Europeans, an expanding book trade, and more opportunities for foreign travel facilitated the elites' introduction to the ideas of the Enlightenment. A selective reading of those ideas buttressed the disenchantment with Iberian rule and provided ready formulae for alternatives. The intellectuals flirted with a political ideology complementary to independence, in most cases republicanism, and economic ideas harmonious with free trade specifically and with emerging capitalism generally. An inclination toward physiocrat doctrine signified a willingness of part of the elites to continue the search for, as well as exploitation and export of, raw materals, the continuation of a well-established pattern of thought and practice of the colonial period which augured poorly for economic independence.

Many of the intellectuals who questioned their Iberian experience while embracing various, varying, and sometimes contradictory Northern European examples held important governmental posts after political independence had been won from Spain and Portugal, while others occupied secondary, but still influential positions in the nascent governments. They found ample opportunity to put their ideas and preferences into practice.

Intensified contacts with Europe throughout the nineteenth century reaffirmed the conclusion reached by many of the elites familiar with the philosophies of the Enlightenment that the Europeans, particularly the English and the French, had confected a desirable civilization worthy of emulation. The opinion of a Bolivian visitor to the continent in 1877, José Avelino Aramayo, that Europe not only represented progress but was needed to foment a similar progress in the New World typified the thought of most of the elites. Aramayo did not hesitate to praise those Latin American nations that most nearly seemed to duplicate Europe. In truth, Europe's rapid industrialization and technological change awed most of the impressionable Latin American cosmopolites who clamored to replicate the process in their own localities, to graft the novelties on the quite different political, social, and economic institutions and realities of the New World. The effort to acquire the outward or material manifestations of the progress they acknowledged as civilization meant that for these Latin Americans in the nineteenth century progress could be measured quantitatively by the amount of exports, the number of steam engines, railroad mileage, or gas lights. The more the capital city architecturally resembled Paris, then *ipso facto* the greater degree of progress that particular country could proclaim. Many a Latin American aristocrat echoed the sigh of the Brazilian Eduardo Prado in the last decade of the century, "Without a doubt the world is Paris."

The ideology of progress in nineteenth-century Latin America was nowhere better expressed than in Argentina by the vocal Generation of 1837, an exceptionally articulate group of liberal intellectuals who bequeathed a formidable literary and political legacy. Their ideas and actions reached far beyond the Argentine frontiers to shape much of the thinking of modern Latin America. Perhaps the intellectuals composing that Generation achieved such an impressive cogency in their writing because they felt they faced a powerful alternative to their preferences in the caudillo Juan Manuel de Rosas, who dominated Argentina from 1829 until 1852. The members of the Generation of 1837 regarded their conflict with Rosas as the struggle between "civilization" and "barbarism," the dichotomy repeatedly invoked by Latin American intellectuals throughout the century. Breathing a fiery religiosity, they perceived their nation to be the victim of that dichotomy, the relentless struggle—most memorable in Augustine's City of God and City of Man—between the opposite natures of people, noble and base, the latter identified with the folk, the former with the elite. In defining civilization, the Generation of 1837 identified the Argentina they intended to create—and in fact did create—as a copy of Europe. In doing so, the members of that generation fastened ideas, thought patterns, and prejudices on Argentina which still remain.

Associated with the port of Buenos Aires, the members of that literary generation looked with horror on the rest of the nation as a vast desert in need of the civilizing hand of Europe. Buenos Aires would serve, according to their blueprint, as a funnel through which European culture would pass on its civilizing mission to redeem the countryside—if it was redeemable. Many of the elite finally concluded it was not and advocated European immigration as the best means to "save" Argentina. In accordance with the political views of the times, those elites aspired to govern Argentina by means of a highly restrictive democracy. Esteban Echeverría summed up that aspiration in his *Dogma Socialista* (1838):

> Collective reason alone is sovereign, not the collective will. This will is blind, capricious, irrational: the will desires; reason examines, weighs, and decides. Thus it happens that the sovereignty of the people can reside only in the reason of the people, and that only the prudent and rational part of the

social community is called to exercise that sovereignty. Those
who are ignorant remain under the tutelage and safeguard of
the laws decreed by the common consent of the men of reason.
Democracy, then, is not the absolute despotism of the masses
or of the majority; it is the rule of reason.

That statement well represented elitist political thought, whether of that generation or later and for that matter whether of
Argentina or elsewhere in Latin America. Some decades later,
as a further example, the Bolivian Félix Avelino Aramayo advocated an aristocratic government "in the Greek sense of the
word," "for" the people but not "by" the people. The experienced and intelligent would be expected to govern for the
greatest benefit of the nation, an ideology complementary to
the earlier beliefs summarized by Echeverría. Indeed, that concept characterized (and still characterizes) most of Latin America. Nothing so extraordinary resided in the nineteenth-century
concept of the few governing the many, but nonetheless it
could prove devastating if the few challenged or changed, intentionally or not, the preferred life-styles of the many and/or
if by miscalculation the few lowered the quality of life of the
majority.

Beyond the confines of the Generation of 1837, the *Dogma
Socialista* achieved neither the acclaim nor the influence of
*Civilización y Barbarie: Vida de Juan Facundo Quiroga (Life
in the Argentine Republic in the Days of the Tyrants: or Civilization and Barbarism)* by Domingo Faustino Sarmiento. First
published in Chile in 1845, where the future Argentine president resided in exile, the book ranks as a major classic of
Argentine literature. It influenced generations of Latin Americans. Emperor Pedro II of Brazil, for one, acknowledged to
Sarmiento the importance he attributed to it. The book set
forth the basic ideology of the dominant elites, a generalization
that sweeps across the nineteenth and well into the twentieth
century. The book denounced a major provincial caudillo,
Juan Facundo Quiroga, who symbolized for Sarmiento the
worst "barbarism" of the vast interior of Argentina. The author
forcefully set forth the dialectic so dear to the hearts of the
Generation of 1837: the progress of the Europeanized city and
the ignorance, barbarism, and primitivism of the countryside.
The gaucho folk society repelled Sarmiento, who observed at
one point, "The nineteenth century and the twelfth century

coexist, the one in the cities; the other in the countryside."
Revealing a general schizophrenia notable in most nineteenth-
century Latin American intellectuals, parts of the book can be
interpreted as sympathetic portraits of rural life and of the typical gaucho types: the trackfinder, the pathfinder, the poet,
and the outlaw. Still, Sarmiento could not accept the rural
populations as the desirable national prototype. He denounced
them for supporting the local caudillos whom they found representative. If they refused to accept the civilization of Europe,
then, Sarmiento advised, European immigrants must be encouraged to repopulate Argentina. Indeed, in his last book,
Conflictos y Armonias de las Razas en América (1883), he
demonstrated that he had imbibed the racist doctrines of nineteenth-century European social scientists to conclude that a
racially mixed population doomed Argentina. All the more
reason, therefore, to cleanse it with "superior" European
blood. Sarmiento represented an extreme, but not unusual
position among his generation by affirming his willingness to
bypass adaptation of European models for Argentina in favor
of the recreation of Europe in Argentina.

Those forceful and influential theses of Sarmiento were neither original nor isolated in the Americas. A year prior to the
publication of the Argentine's rural-urban dialectic, for example, Francisco Bilbao published in Santiago his own analysis of
Chilean society, *Sociabilidad Chilena,* which equated the countryside with tradition and the cities with progress. The inhabitant of the countryside was "barbaric," while the city dweller
radiated "culture." The Chilean described the *guasos* (cow-
boys) in a schizoid manner foreshadowing Sarmiento's treatment of the gaucho: spirited, strong, confident but nonetheless
"barbaric." Also similar to the better known work of the Argentine, Bilbao prescribed education and European immigration
as the certain means to "civilize" the nation. Indeed,
everywhere throughout Latin America, the elites proclaimed
their mission to introduce civilization. They felt embattled.
They feared the barbaric masses might engulf them and drown
their cherished civlization. In his report to the legislature of the
frontier province of Goiás, Brazil, in 1845, the president of the
province, José de Assiz Mascarenhas, decried the threat of Indian barbarism, which threatened the "civilized population."
Although he respected the efforts to Christianize those Indians,

he judged "force" to be equally necessary to protect civilization from the barbarians. The governor of Jalisco, Mexico, Ignácio Luis Vallarta, vividly described similar threats in 1873. Condemning the popular Lozada movement, he warned, "Peaceful and civilized society has begun to suffer in some of the municipalities of this state attacks from the turbulent and barbaric hordes of the Álica Mountains, who inflict the ferocity of their instincts, the rapacity of their customs, and their wicked schemes." A spectre of "American barbarism" haunted the European-oriented cities.

The best-known Argentine novel of the nineteenth century, *Amalia* (translated into English under the same title), further propagated the attitudes of the Generation of 1837. Considered by many a prototype of Argentine Romanticism, it appeared first in a serialized form; the complete novel was published in 1855. Its author, José Mármol, castigated the caudillo Rosas as a tyrant, the fitting representative of rural barbarism. The main protagonists were drawn from the capital's aristocracy, European in dress, thought, and action, a sharp contrast with the rustic supporters of the caudillo, who were depicted as the incarnation of evil. Further, an open racism characterized the novel: the persecuted aristocracy was white, thus of pure European lineage and obviously "civilized"; the supporters of Rosas were a disagreeable and cruel lot of "mongrels"; mulatto, mestizo, or racially mixed in one way or another, and of course equated with inferiority and barbarism. *Amalia*, like *Civilización y Barbarie* and *Dogma Socialista*, represented the outlook and mentality of a generation instrumental in the shaping of Argentina in the nineteenth century. Indeed, two participants in that movement, Bartolomé Mitre and Sarmiento, served successively as presidents of Argentina, 1862–1868 and 1868–1874, crucial years in the formation of that nation. Modern Argentina heavily bears their imprint.

The interplay of countryside and city absorbed the attention of the literati throughout Latin America, who frequently made it a theme of their novels and stories. Accelerating urbanization was, after all, a major trend of the century, but also the association of the city with progress was inevitable. The Chilean novelist Alberto Blest Gana treated perceptively the interplay of rural and urban in his *Martín Rivas* (1862). The author at one point spoke of "the strange looking provincials" and always considered them as real bumpkins. The young Rivas, innocent, even puritanical, left the provinces for the city where he was changed, "civilized" as it were. Not inappropriate to the times, Blest Gana offered the formula for upward mobility. His novel of class interests (and conflicts) depicted the two acceptable means for the ambitious to improve their lot: through skill, intelligence, education, and hard work, or through a fortuitous marriage. Martín Rivas combined both to transform himself from an impoverished provincial to a respected member of the urban elite. Blest Gana might picture the nobility of the countryside, but it still remained rustic; the city might appear corrupt, but it radiated culture. The novel subtly traced the Europeanization of the virtuous Rivas, depicting what appeared to the novelist and reading public at the time as both inevitable and desirable.

Intellectuals did not have to be hostile to local or native American cultures to advocate Europeanization of the New World. Their own Europeanization blinded most of them to any alternative. Such minds revealed a greater intellectual complexity requiring more refined psychological interpretations. Much of what they said was predictable, a part of the intellectual formula of the times, but they were also moving away from the dogmatism characteristic of the ideology of the Generation of 1837 toward a vital questioning of their environment, which later led to an intellectual diversity, part of which denied the cosmopolitan outlook of the Generation of 1837 and its hemispheric sympathizers. The Peruvian novelist Clorinda Matto de Turner exemplified that group. Her *Aves sin Nido (Birds without a Nest)* (1889) widely acclaimed as the first novel in defense of the Indians, denounced in convincing prose the abuse and exploitation of the Peruvian Indians. She nobly expressed her reasons for writing the novel as four: to call attention to the suffering of the Indians, to urge the reform of backward conditions in the Peruvian interior, to suggest the progress that must be made, and to help create a Peruvian literature. Appropriately in the preface to third edition (1889), Emilio Gutierrez de Quintanilla considered a major theme of the novel to be "civilization versus barbarism." Whereas the Spaniards should have introduced civilization in the Andes, they were responsible for enslaving and debasing the Indians, returning them to "the barbarism of the primitive past." The

Republic had the responsibility of redeeming the Indians through "education, employment, and equality." Neither he nor Matto de Turner suggested that the Indians might find redemption through recourse to their own past values; both recommended a Europeanized future for them.

For Matto de Turner, the city symbolized the civilization needed to regenerate Peru. More than one inhabitant of the remote village of Kíllac affirmed that the future lay in the city. As Manuel, one of the novel's principal characters, remarked, "All those who have sufficient means migrate to the centers of civilization." Lima was presented in the novel as such a center. Speaking to two young girls on their way to the Peruvian capital for the first time, Manuel declared enthusiastically, "Oh yes, Lima! There the heart becomes educated and the mind instructed. . . . To travel to Lima is to go to heaven's antechamber and to see from there the throne of the Glory of the Future. They say that our beautiful capital is a fairytale city." If one could move on to a European city the satisfaction would increase. Fernando Marín promised to take his wife from Kíllac to Lima and then capped his promise with the announcement that from there they would visit Europe. A train transported those villagers from the rural past to the urban future. Fittingly, the train's engineer was an Englishman.

While Matto de Turner vividly denounced the barbarity of village life and graphically portrayed the injustices inflicted on the Indians, she was vague in offering solutions for the debasement of the Indians other than migration to Lima, a solution that resolved few if any problems for millions of Indians over the centuries. She expressed a firm and typical, although ill-defined, hope that education would provide some answers, the most universally proffered solution since the Enlightenment, and evinced a general vagueness that somehow "pure Christianity" — never defined but certainly intended to be the opposite of the corrupt Catholicism she denounced in the novel — would uplift the Peruvians. Of course the religion she preferred was European in origin just as the education she advocated would inculcate the finest European values. Both guaranteed the cultural genocide of the majority. The conclusion deduced from the novel was that if Europe debased the Indians, Europe could also redeem them. In her refusal to find any local solutions and her insistence on Europeanization of the Incas, Matto de Turner resembled Sarmiento. Although nearly half a century separated *Aves sin Nido* from *Civilización y Barbarie,* the ideology advocating European solutions to local problems in both books coincided. However, a major difference, and it is a significant one, separated the philosophy of the two: Matto de Turner blamed Europe for the "barbarization" of the Incas just as she believed Europe would "civilize" them. On a very basic level, fundamental to her humanism, she defended the Indians' right to exist. Nowhere do we find in her many works the dogmatism of Sarmiento, which demanded the locals "shape up" or give way to European immigrants.

The schizophrenia characteristic of the nineteenth-century intellectuals and consequently of their nationalism was acutely apparent in a writer-philosopher of the stature of Euclides da Cunha. His masterpiece, *Os Sertões* (1902), admirably translated into English as *Rebellion in the Backlands,* ranks as a major classic in Latin American literature, worthy of a place of honor in world literature. Comte, Darwin, Spencer, and a host of other European mentors left their mark on da Cunha who faithfully included their ideas in his analysis of his native land. Yet, his book revealed a subtle or troubled questioning of those European theories, a daring stance for a Latin American intellectual at the end of the nineteenth century. Indeed, da Cunha's mind must have been a turmoil of struggle between sacrosanct European theory and his own perceptive observations on Brazil, so much so that in a later edition of his book he added some extraordinary footnotes indicating his inclination more toward observation and thus away from exotic European theories.

As a journalist, da Cunha accompanied the federal army into the *sertão,* the backlands, of Bahia in 1897 on its mission to exterminate the defiant followers of the religious mystic Antônio Conselheiro at Canudos. That complex figure emerged on one level as a leader of a millenarian movement of awesome potential and on another level can be interpreted as an activist populist leader urging the poor to refuse to pay the new taxes levied on them by a distant government. The impoverished inhabitants of Brazil's arid Northeastern interior flocked to Antônio Conselheiro, who represented to them a guide (a savior) who would lead them into a promised land. He offered the hope of which their lives were destitute. By the thousands they settled in the rustic settlement he established at Canudos. He exercised a political, economic, and religious power whose appeal to the masses unnerved the elites. The state and federal governments, as well as the religious hierarchy, regarded him and his settlement at Canudos as a threat to be eliminated promptly. The expeditions to accomplish that goal represented the cities in their determination to subdue the countryside. A comfortable life in the cities near the coast did not prepare da Cunha for what he witnessed in the interior. The different types of people, customs, topography, even the differently spoken Portuguese astounded him. He felt that he had been transported "outside Brazil." The existence of "two societies" within a single nation caused him to reflect at great length on which was the real Brazil. He resolved his perplexity in favor of the poor but strong people of the hinterlands, whom he eventually classifed as "the very core of our nationality, the bedrock of our race." He characterized their society as "the vigorous core of our national life." The shock of discovering a new and different Brazil never dissipated. Some years after the publication of the first edition of his book, obviously after much reflection and no little agony, he reinforced his previous conclusions:

> I did encounter in the backlands type an ethnic subcategory already formed and one which, as a result of historical conditions, had been freed of the exigencies of a borrowed civilization such as would have hindered its definitive evolution. This is equivalent to saying that in that indefinable compound — the Brazilian — I came upon something that was stable, a point of reference reminiscent of the integrating molecule in the initial stage of crystallization. And it was natural enough that, once having admitted the bold and inspiring conjecture that we are destined to national unity, I should have seen in those sturdy *caboclos* the hardy nucleus of our future, the bedrock of our race. . . .

> As we make our way deeper into the land . . . the pure white, the pure Negro, and the pure Indian are now a rarity. The generalized miscegenation, meanwhile, has given rise to every variety of racial crossing; but, as we continue on our way, these shadings tend to disappear, and there is to be seen a greater uniformity of physical and moral characteristics. In brief, we have struck bedrock — in the man of the backlands.

Da Cunha's discovery disturbed most of the educated public, which still clung to its revered European images.

Da Cunha found himself in an agonizing dilemma over his admiration for the people of the interior and his European indoctrination. The book weakened — although it consistently adhered to realism — when the author resolved that the city must triumph over the countryside, Europeanization over Brazilianization. He proposed education as a weapon more powerful than cannons to subjugate the rebellious backlanders to the city. He found the justification for the war, then, to be the mission to carry civilization into the hinterlands. At one point he wrote:

> The entire campaign would be a crime, a futile and a barbarous one, if we were not to take advantage of the paths opened by our artillery, by following up our cannon with a constant, stubborn, and persistent campaign of education, with the object of drawing these rude and backward fellow countrymen of ours into the current of our times and of our national life. . . . Our biological evolution demands the guarantee of social evolution. We are condemned to civilization. Either we shall progress or we shall perish. So much is certain and our choice clear.

Thus, for all its nationalism and insight, *Os Sertões* finally aligned itself with the forces of Europeanization. Da Cunha was a social Darwinist, who understood that the people of the interior, victims of aggression and injustice, must succumb to the advance of "progress." By supporting the city as civilization over the countryside as barbarity, *Os Sertões* in the final analysis bore a close relationship to *Civilización y Barbarie,* although perhaps da Cunha maintained an ambivalence uncharacteristic of Sarmiento.

It was not the urban-rural dichotomy alone which preoccupied most of da Cunha's contemporaries. They viewed the question of civilization versus barbarism in racial terms also and subscribed to the European racial doctrines of the day, which ranked the Aryan and Anglo at the pinnacle of civilization while regarding the Africans and Indians as real obstacles to progress. A mixture of the European with either the Indian or black was regarded — as European social doctrine prescribed — as a sure condemnation to an inferior status. A leading cultural review published in Rio de Janeiro in 1895, *Dom Quixote,* castigated the Brazilian "race" composed of the "backward" African, "decadent" Portuguese, and "primitive" Indian. The author's recommendation was standard for the times: "What we need are new forces, originating in the strong and vigorous races that on arrival here will work by absorption to improve our race." Rather than a novelty, the article simply recapitulated and reemphasized an idea current for at least half a century among the coastal elites. The Brazilian intellectuals put great faith in the "bleaching process," the eradication of the "weak" Indian and African genes by the "stronger," more "dominant" European ones. The theory might not have squared with European anthropological thought, but it provided a necessary solution for the distraught Brazilian elite and according to its proponents offered the surest method to reproduce European civilization in their vast nation. Harmonious with similar hopes in Argentina and elsewhere, the intellectuals despaired of remolding the local populations and so planned to replace them. By midcentury, the Indians had withdrawn into the Amazonian hinterlands, and the prohibition of the slave trade had stopped the African inflow. The government threw open the doors to European immigration, which in fact did change the physical topology of the Brazilian.

The intellectuals of Indo-America demonstrated no greater understanding or tolerance of the Indians than their Brazilian counterparts did of the Africans. The huge Indian populations of Mexico, Guatemala, Ecuador, Peru, Bolivia, and Paraguay embarrassed the intellectuals, who regarded them as barbaric at worst and childlike creatures at best. The Indians' disdain of European civilization only intensified the suspicions of the elites. Governments and landowners felt perfectly correct in forcing the Indians to labor for them under the rationalization that it fostered contact with the elites and thus exposed the Indians to the indubitable benefits of European civilization. Whatever their professed political suasion, the Latin American elites seldom shied away from exploiting the Indians.

The Mexican intellectuals vigorously debated the "Indian problem" in the nineteenth century, a debate that accelerated during the long government of Porfirio Díaz (1876–1911), whose policies divested the Indian communities of several million acres and literally enslaved entire Indian groups. The intellectuals divided over the intelligence and ability of the Indians as well as the feasibility of integrating them into national life, that is, making Europeanized Mexicans of the indigenous inhabitants. One side emphasized the potential of the Indians and urged the government to improve their conditions. Intellectuals like Justo Sierra believed education and greater exposure to Westernization while rescuing the Indians would transform them into mestizo Mexicans. To others, however, the Indians constituted an insuperable obstacle to national progress; they particularly decried their communal spirit and lack of individualism. Writing in the 1860s, Antonio García Cubas identified the Indians as the "enemy" of other Mexicans and predicted their "decadence and degeneration" could not be reversed. Decades later, Francisco Bulnes, the quintessential Social Darwinist, published his blunt and influential *El Porvenir de las Naciones Hispano-Americanas* (1899), which concluded that the racial inferiority of the Indians prohibited national development. The almost universal solution to the "Indian problem" advocated the encouragement of European immigration with the hope that the new blood would dilute the Indian. The debates focused exclusively on whether or not the Indians could be Europeanized. The intellectuals entertained no other alternatives. None recognized that the Indians might want to draw on their own past rather than Europe's or perceived any attributes in the Indian community worthy of incorporation into the national ethos.

A somewhat different debate on the Indians took place in Guatemala City in 1893 at the Congreso Pedagógico Centroamericano, whose first topic for discussion was, "What would be the most efficient method of civilizing the Indian race in order to imbue it with the ideas of progress and the habits of cultured peoples?" In a preliminary study for the congress, the Guatemalan Juan Fernández Ferraz rejected the idea that the Indians were condemned to backwardness and eventual extinction. As one Honduran delegate, Professor Alberto Membreno, noted, the Organization Committee of the Congress left no doubt that the Indians possessed the aptitude for "civilization." The question before the congress revolved around *how* to civilize them. The delegates roundly condemned the racism prevalent in the hemisphere which hastened the extinction of the native population and castigated both the United States and Argentina for genocide. In a very perceptive speech, Ferraz denounced the alienation of the Indians from their own environment and advised that the first step toward helping them would be the return of their lands. Although the Central American intellectuals showed a far greater understanding of the problems and a more perceptive insight into the Indian mentality than their Mexican counterparts at a similar time, they, too, saw Europeanization as the ultimate fate of the Indians. Unlike many of their Mexican colleagues, however, the Central Americans judged the native population intellectually capable of adopting European ways.

While the Mexican and Central American intellectuals debated national Indian policies, the Argentine government aggressively pursued its own policy of genocide. In the so-called Conquest of the Desert, 1879–80, the army under the command of General Julio A. Roca, who later served twice as president, fanned out across the pampas to clear the land of Indians once and for all. In an Order of the Day to his troops dated April 26, 1879, General Roca left no doubt in the minds of the soldiers of their exalted duty to the fatherland, a fatherland that seemed to have no place for the original inhabitants. These few sentences from the Order revealed the full intentions of the government in Buenos Aires:

> When the wave of humanity invades these desolate fields that were yesterday the state of sanguinary and devastating raids to turn them into markets of wealth and flourishing towns, in which millions of men may live rich and happy—then and not till then the true worth of your efforts will be perceived. Destroying these nests of land pirates and taking possession of the vast region that shelters them, you have opened and widened the horizons of your country toward the southland, tracing as it were with your bayonets an immense field for the development of future greatness.

The armies massacred Indians; a few succeeded in escaping to the Patagonian wilderness; others were absorbed into the rural work force. Those campaigns in fact did open up vast tracts of new territory. How much they contributed to the well-being of the majority, however, is problematic. The lands promptly fell under the control of rich *hacendados,* most of whom were intimately linked to the export economy and partners in the exploitation of an increasingly dependent Argentina. For those privileged few, the public funds that financed the military

campaigns proved an ideal means to expand their landholdings. For the government, the army conveniently served as the
executioner of those remaining "barbarians" who continued to
reject Europeanization.

The countryside increasingly dependent on exports to insure prosperity, whether in Argentina or elsewhere in Latin
America, was perfectly mirrored in the cities, whose life and
looks depended to a large degree on those exports and the imports they facilitated. Those cities with their cafes, shops,
theaters, operas, balls, and academies often opulently pack-
aged in Beaux Arts architecture absorbed the attention of the
elites and to an ever larger degree symbolized their nations to
them. Although technology appealed the most to the elites,
they also aped certain life-styles and professed the values accompanying them. The result was to graft onto Latin America
those accoutrements of progress as the elites perceived it rather
than to accommodate new ideas and modes by reforming the
basic national institutions or to modify the new ways to complement older institutions.

Both a contributor to and the consequence of a dependent
economy, cosmetic modernization further subordinated Latin
American political behavior to North Atlantic demands and
degraded auchtonomous cultures to accommodate imported
ones. Many of these results had not been entertained by the intellectuals who wrote so glowingly of progress.

The elites steadfastly pursued their vision of progress. In
their pursuit, they readily understood the need to guarantee
order and stability, peace and security in order to receive the
loans, investments, technology, and immigration they required
to maintain or enhance their life-styles. Thus many of their activities and decisions were more for international approval than
internal improvement. To meet the costs of modernization,
commercial agriculture and mining—the export sector—received priorities in attention and investment. By midcentury,
the plans and policies of most governments clearly reflected
those realities. President Tomás Cipriano de Mosquera of Colombia (1845-49) supported a program of road building, steam
navigation on the Magdalena River, increased tobacco exports,
and invitations to foreign technicians. By the 1850s, the imperial government of Brazil had embarked on a program to

encourage railroad construction, foster steam navigation, reorganize banking, favor increased coffee exports, and entice European immigrants. A reform manifesto in Mexico in 1859 called for encouraging foreign immigration, capital, and technology, the restoration of law and order, renovation of mining, growth of commerce, and nationalization of Church property. The government of President Domingo F. Sarmiento of Argentina (1868-74) imposed order, opened the doors to immigrants, built schools, pushed the railroad into the pampas, and in general facilitated foreign trade. While all of the activities might have contributed to development, few if any did in practice. Rather, they served to strengthen the dynamic, but dangerous export sector of the economy and in so doing also deepened dependency.

By the last quarter of the century, the governments slowly expanded their economic interests to include industrialization, whose first stages concentrated on the consumer items demanded by the elites and the emerging middle class. As it took shape, industrialization increased foreign domination of national economies. The foreigners sold the Latin Americans the machinery their new industries required and thus earned profits; they invested in the industrialization to augment those profits; they loaned money to fledgling Latin American entrepreneurs and earned interest; foreign technicians often supervised the running of the new machinery and earned salaries. The result was a substantial outflow of currency to create industries that benefited only a few. Nonetheless, to that small minority who controlled the governments, the benefits appeared to outweigh the expenses. Possibly they did not yet understand the ultimate consequences of their policies: deepening dependency. Or, if they did, they seemed to regard the price worthy of their well-being. The concept of progress as the emulation of Northern Europe and the United States triumphed. It did not seem to matter that the vast majority of the Latin Americans received no benefits from it. In theory, at least, all were to benefit in due time. While the countryside was regarded as hopelessly backward, the ruling—and increasingly urban—elites tolerated it, realizing that to tamper with the basic rural institutions would threaten a system that, if not perfect, still could be manipulated to favor them.

CHAPTER THREE

The Preservation and Glorification of the Elite Preference

History perpetuated the views of the elites and rationalized their political and economic choices as logical, preserving for a long time a one-dimensional view of the nineteenth century. Thus, the pursuit of rapid Europeanization emerged as a dominant historical theme; historians dwelt on the visible manifestations of material change; their studies lauded those leaders who facilitated "progress," frequently according them the accolades of heroes. The reasons for that historiographical conformity are not difficult to find. Historians impose on society a perception of the past shaped by the topics they study, the values they hold, and their interpretations. When historians represent a relatively homogeneous group, their histories tend to perpetuate a similarity by ascribing to the past a uniformity more harmonious with the class vision than with the totality of experience. Such restrictions characterized nineteenth-century Latin American historiography.

A study of the biographies of sixty-three historians active in the nineteenth century permits the sketching of a tentative composite profile from which individual variance was slight. Sixty-two were males. Almost all boasted a secondary school education or the equivalent, and most received advanced training in a university, military school, or seminary. Law degrees predominated. Their educations closely resembled those of their European peers. Most of them spoke French and a considerable number added English and/or German to their linguistic repertory. Indeed their knowledge of foreign languages in some cases was extraordinary. João Capistrano de Abreu read French, English, and German, as well as Latin; Bartolomé Mitre knew English, French, Italian, and Latin; Pedro Paz Soldán y Unánue mastered French, English, and German. A few wrote with admirable grace of style in the foreign languages of their preference. Joaquim Nabuco, for example, wrote elegantly in French and commendably in English. He authored several of his works directly in those languages. These historians were by no means exceptional in their language skills. Although the historians relied on their languages to faciliate their foreign travels they used them principally to gain direct access to European authors. Charles Darwin, Herbert Spencer, Auguste Comte, Leopold von Ranke, Freidrich Ratzel, François Pierre Guillaume Guizot, Jules Michelet, Thomas B. Macaulay, Henry Thomas Buckle, Thomas Carlyle, as well as the philosophes of the European Enlightenment, absorbed the most attention of the Latin American historians.

The familiarity of the Latin American historians with European ideas is readily evident in their biases and quotations. They had read both the classic and contemporary European historians whom they quoted with ease as well as admiration. They deferred to European authorities to settle any disputes. When writing on historiographical topics, the Latin Americans drew heavily from Old World sources and examples. In consulting many of their essays, the reader notes an almost total absence of any references to Latin America. Cecilio Acosta authored an essay with the appealing title "Influencia del Elemento Histórico-político en la Literatura Dramática y en la Novela," a hundred pages discussing major and minor European savants without linking his important topic to anything in his native Venezuela, or in Latin America for that matter.

Only hesitantly and occasionally did Latin Americans question the European masters and turn inward or to each other for inspiration. Contrary to the currents of his times, Andrés Bello in 1845 cautioned that while European historiography offered "a model, a guide, a method," it could not provide the "philosophy" to interpret New World history. By the end of the century, some evidence does exist of a greater circulation of ideas among the Latin American historians themselves. Discoursing on "La Historia" at the University of San Carlos in Guatemala City in 1900, Rafael Montúfar displayed the usual intimate knowledge of European historiography but then went on to praise the Chilean intellectual Valentín Letelier and in particular his *La Evolución de la Historia* (2d ed., 1900), a confection of Henry Thomas Buckle's orientation with Comtean philosophy spiced with ideas from Spencer and Stuart Mill. Sympathetic to the Chilean's positivist approach to history, the Guatemalan commended his depreciation of history's inclusion of tradition, mythology, and legend and his insistence on "facts" in a sociological view of the past. As previously mentioned, D. F. Sarmiento's *Civilización y Barbarie* ranked as one historical work that exercised a profound influence throughout Latin America.

While it is difficult to indicate the precise class standing of all of these sixty-three historians, it is nonetheless true that all enjoyed privileges in a society that afforded few. If not born into the ranks of the wealthiest families, they lived comfortable lives more akin to the life-styles of the upper class than to the humble status of the majority. They associated and identified with the social, political, and economic elites. The pursuit of history assumed the availability of leisure time. Their longevity further testifies to their pleasant life-styles. Their ages at death averaged more than sixty years in a society where half that life-span was more nearly normal. Such longevity speaks well of their diet, medical care, and routine. Further, almost all of them were of pure or nearly pure European lineage. None conceded any recent African descent, and those with Indian ancestors chose to prune rather than cultivate that branch of the family tree.

As a group these historians looked fondly to a European heritage, for themselves and their countries as well. The Chilean Francisco Bilbao unabashedly pronounced non-Iberian Europe to be the future of Latin America. He was even more specific: "The new age has dawned in France." In addition to reading about and admiring Europe, discussing the Old World, and aping continental styles, the historians knew it first hand. They tended to be a well-traveled group. Some resided in Europe, preferably in Paris, for extended periods; others studied there; still others served there as diplomats; while most of them made the "grand tour" at least once. They coveted, and some received, European recognition. Elected to the Academy of Sciences of Paris in 1882, Diego Barros Arana was awarded what most Latin American intellectuals considered the ultimate accolade. Toward the end of the century, their travels broadened to include the Western Hemisphere. A representative number visited the United States or other Latin American nations. A few included both.

With rare exceptions, the historians resided in the capitals, partly because of the educational and cultural advantages but also, significantly, because most of them were connected at one time or another, in one way or another with the governments. They held a variety of bureaucratic posts, some served as legislators, judges, and ministers, and a couple even as presidents, while still others unsuccessfully sought that exalted office. A representative sampling of their governmental careers reveals that the Mexican Lucas Alamán held the portfolio of minister of foreign relations on three occasions; Lorenzo Montúfar carried out numerous diplomatic missions and was both minister of foreign relations and of education in Costa Rica; Joaquim Nabuco, three times elected to the Chamber of Deputies, later represented Brazil as minister to the Court of St. James and then as ambassador to the United States; Vicente G. Quesada was an Argentine federal deputy representing Corrientes and later an ambassador; Vicente Riva Palacio governed both the states of Mexico and Michoacán; Ramón Sotomayor y Valdés represented Chile first as minister to Mexico and then to Bolivia before being elected to the Chamber of Deputies and later appointed official clerk of the Ministery of the Treasury. Few could surpass the number of public positions held by Brazil's Francisco Inácio Marcondes Homem de Melo in local, provincial, and national governments. Among others, he served as president of the provinces of São Paulo, Ceará, Rio Grande do Sul, and Bahia; as deputy in the Chamber of Deputies; as Director of the Bank of Brazil; and as minister of the empire as well as minister of war. The many burdens of public office never prevented him from teaching and writing history nor detracted from active participation in the Instituto Histórico e Geográfico Brasileiro.

Obviously the people who wrote Latin American history in

the last century were not passive observers and recorders of their class or society. As members of a minute elite in those new countries, they divided their attention among myriad interests and responsibilities. Most significantly, they played active roles in shaping and administering national institutions. Not surprisingly then, they displayed a loyalty to the official institutions of which they formed such an integral part. Such integration into and loyalty to the institutions shaped their historical "world view" as apologists rather than critics. Few, if any, earned their livelihoods exclusively as historians. Indeed, in twentieth-century terms, few could qualify as "professional historians," although by the end of the century some did enjoy state appointments directing archives or libraries or teaching history in prestigious national institutes, which permitted them to devote more of their time to history.

Life in the capital cities definitely shaped their views, so much so that some of the national histories they wrote were little more than chronicles of the events in the principal city. The capitals often communicated more quickly with Paris and London than with the hinterlands of their own countries. For geographic as well as cultural reasons, the historians were more attuned to the metropolis than to the life-styles and preferences of their rural compatriots. As noted in the previous chapter, Euclydes da Cunha's "discovery" of the *sertão* of Brazil traumatized him. There was a Brazil the urbanized intellectual never even imagined. Others, raised in the interior, like D. F. Sarmiento, fled to the capital and denounced the "backwardness" of the provinces. Still others, like the young Rufino Blanco Fombona of Venezuela, tried to expose themselves to rural life only to be bored or disillusioned: "The slowness and rusticity of the peasants exasperates me. They are always wrong and it is impossible that they should ever be rescued from their sad condition of inferior beings except through a persistent educational programme. . . . I cannot talk to any of them for more than five minutes at a time. I can find nothing to say to them." Such attitudes isolated most of the historians from national reality and certainly from the majority of their fellow citizens. Consciously or unconsciously they dwelt on their class and the national capital as though they constituted the nation. Thus, they projected through their histories the life-style of the minority as though it represented the majority, an extrapolation that might skew the perceptions of the unwary reader of their histories.

In accordance with the elitist dictates of the time, the historians applauded rule by the "enlightened," a concept that disenfranchised all but a few. The propertied and/or literate constituted that select group. The colonial past attracted considerable attention from them, but they seem to have written as much, perhaps more, about their own century, revealing a strong "contemporary orientation." They wrote primarily political history and biographies, a logical selection considering the times. As late as the 1880s, the noted Argentine historian Vicente Fidel López declared, "Argentine history is only and exclusively political history." The ruling elite felt obliged to justify the new national institutions and the course of events shaped by independence. The historians did just that, often by eulogizing individuals whose life-styles harmonized with the goals and ideas of the elite. Januário da Cunha Barbosa, one of the founders of the Instituto Histórico e Geográfico Brasileiro in 1838, offered a formula followed for the rest of the century: "To know the biographies of all the outstanding men of any period is to know the history of those times." Indeed, it became difficult to escape the "great men" approach to history. The writings of Bartolomé Mitre provide one of myriad examples. In his two major works, *Historia de Belgrano y de la Independencia Argentina* (2 vols., 1858-59) and *Historia de San Martín de la Emancipación Sud-Americana* (3 vols., 1887-88), he viewed both national and South American independence as the consequence of extraordinary individuals who contributed more than their share to effect those momentous events. In his *História Geral do Brasil* (2 vols., 1854-57), Francisco Adolfo de Varnhagen did not conceal his contempt for the "vil população." He denigrated rebels, nonconformists, and the masses alike. Their influence on the course of events, if any, was negative. Great men shaped history, and none had contributed more to Brazil's destiny than those of the ruling House of Braganza. Lucas Alamán expressed similar ideas in his disdain for popular participation in the political process as well as in his preference for a monarchy. His monumental *Historia de Méjico* (5 vols., 1849-52) did not consider the movement led by Miguel Hidalgo and José María Morelos as a contribution toward independence but rather as an attack on "property and civilization." The creole elites effected independence in accordance with Alamán's interpretation, and Iturbide emerged as the embodiment of orderly transition to nationhood for Mexico. Chilean historians displayed a similar bias for the individual whose exemplary life offered a moral and patriotic model for the nation. So compelling was the urge to ferret out and glorify great men that Diego Barros Arana conceded, "If history does not offer us model men, it is the duty of the historian to make them." Benjamín Vicuña Mackenna determined to write a "history of the people," but his *Historia General de la República de Chile* (5 vols., 1866–83) reveals that he succumbed to the usual temptations and produced instead a "history of the heroes." The aspirations to write broader histories, while not lacking, were seldom realized. Elitist historians selected representatives of their own Europeanized class as heroes to be envied, honored, and, if possible, emulated by all.

In their own eyes, the historians of the new nations assumed a heavy responsibility: to arouse the patriotism of their compatriots. Januário da Cunha Barbosa piously predicted, "The love of national glory will lead us to cleanse our history of inaccuracies." Then he asked rhetorically, "And will not a truthful history of our country offer the lessons that can so profitably be used by Brazilian citizens in the performance of their important duties?" In 1845, Vicente Fidel López informed the Faculty of Philosophy and Humanities of Santiago, during a lecture, "The goal of history is to teach men to live as good patriots of their nation; to learn the virtues of a citizen; to defend what is right on all occasions; and to know the desires of the state and try to fulfill them as best they can." Chilean historians apparently heeded the advice. Through lectures, writing, example, and political position, they molded civic values and prescribed future development. They not only wrote the past, they formulated the future. And they left no doubt that it was to be a Europeanized future. To Lucas Alamán, too, history was more than the recreation of the past: it served as a guide for the future. Whatever patriotic lessons history might teach, the historians drew inevitably and exclusively from the activities of the elites. In the case of Brazilian historians, for example, they chose to elevate Joaquim José da Silva Xavier, better known by his nickname, Tiradentes, to the summit as national hero. In the ill-fated and equally ill-conceived and vaguely defined Minas Conspiracy, 1788–89, against Portuguese rule, he emerged as a principal plotter for which the authorities condemned him to death. Tiradentes, by the way, represented the colonial elites, a white male of substance and standing. For the much more revolutionary Bahian Conspiracy of 1798, four blacks were convicted and executed. Those subverters of Portuguese rule were humble folk. Until well into the twentieth century, historians ignored both them and their conspiracy. Tiradentes continues to be the national hero. Shelves sag under the numerous biographies of him. Yet, to this day, not one biography exists of any of Bahia's black conspirators.

For sources, the historians relied on public and private libraries, the latter more frequently than the former. The historians were bibliophiles, each forming his own collection around the topics that most attracted him. They used public and private archives, but the haphazard storage of documents, few of which were cataloged, greatly complicated, if it did not discourage, research. From its inception, the Instituto Histórico e Geográfico Brasileiro strove to collect, organize, and preserve documentation. Further, it, as well as the imperial government, commissioned various Brazilians to locate and copy pertinent manuscripts in foreign archives. Varnhagen discovered some fundamental documents for Brazilian history in the Portuguese and Spanish archives and extended his research to many of the other major European archives as well as to many in South America. Probably no one surpassed José Toribio Medina in the collection of documents. During several visits to Europe, particularly to Spain, the Chilean scholar copied thousands of manuscripts relating to Latin American history, which he later published. Some of the historians were acquainted with the families of the principal actors in the national drama and gained access to those private papers. Some witnessed or even participated in the events they described. Gabriel René Moreno might well typify the determined historian in search of varied documentation. The Bolivian historian enthusiastically collected books, pamphlets, and periodicals and incessantly copied manuscripts. In his youth, he interviewed the surviving leaders of the Revolution of 1809 and incorporated their accounts into his work. His travels to Lima, Buenos Aires, and

Europe as well as his long residency in Santiago provided the bibliophile excellent opportunities to expand his library and explore archives, which yielded rich details for his reconstruction of Bolivia's past. Moreno, like his counterparts in all of Latin America during the last century, relied most heavily for his source material on libraries and archives, which, in the final analysis were repositories for the books and papers of the elites. Consequently the major sources available to the historians — or perhaps the sources the historians chose to use most frequently — only reinforced their own elitist tendencies.

Historians of liberal, conservative, romantic, and positivist persuasions debated among themselves, sometimes acrimoniously. As one scholar of nineteenth-century Uruguayan historiography, Juan Antonio Oddone, emphasized, history was "an ideological arsenal" from which its practitioners drew whatever arms they needed to defend their cause. Disagreements flared as to whether emphasis should fall on documentation or interpretation. Some argued the facts spoke for themselves, while others relied on intuition, imagination, and insight to compose their studies of the past. Not a few saw the hand of God writ large and ascribed much causation to Divine Providence. Federico González Suárez affirmed, "Divine Providence and Human Liberty are the fundamentals evident in History. Without losing sight for an instant of the providential destiny of nations, History relates their vicissitudes through time demonstrating how they have fulfilled that inviolable Law of Providence." At the opposite extreme, the positivist historians scoffed at the idea of such supernatural interventions in human activities, but did not hesitate to castigate the Roman Catholic Church for most of the national problems as they perceived them.

Although historians regarded their nations as the products of Europe, they could not entirely escape questions of Indian and African input. Here, of course, European racial doctrines shaped their views — and must have generated many psychoses. A German historian, Karl Friedrich Philipp von Martius, introduced in 1843 the fascinating theme of the contributions of the three races to the formation of Brazil, but his ideas did not have an impact on Brazilian historiography for nearly a century. For nationalistic reasons, the Indian assumed a special significance and raised some thorny ideological problems. The role of the Indian in Brazilian history incited sporadic discussion. In fact, debate of some substance revolved around the proper historiographical treatment to be accorded the Indians and precipitated a stormy exchange between João Francisco Lisboa and Varnhagen at midcentury. Significantly, Lisboa spent most of his life in his natal São Luís do Maranhão and thus represented those few historians who resided in the provinces in the nineteenth century but still managed to have a national impact, while Varnhagen, intimately associated with the court in Rio de Janeiro, spent most of his life abroad. The historians often came to terms with the question of what to do with the Indians in history by envisioning the noble Indian, an Indian prince who looked, acted, thought, and talked like a European. The idealized and romanticized Indian was acceptable as a symbol.

Questions of interpretation absorbed much of the historians' attention and seemingly incited the most debate, at least some of the most excited debate. Into those debates often intruded the liberal and conservative political perspectives for those historians were in no way apolitical. One of the major historical controversies occurred in Mexico and pitted the Conservatives, brilliantly represented by Lucas Alamán, against the Liberals, rather more ambiguously represented by José María Luis Mora. Alamán asserted that Hernán Cortés founded the Mexican nation and that the long colonial period had benefited Mexico. In looking to the Spanish past, Alamán differed markedly from most historians of Spanish-speaking Latin America, but in overlooking — indeed, denigrating — the Indian heritage he was well within the trends of nineteenth-century historiography. In sum, Alamán, too, looked to Europe but, unusual for his century, more to Spain than to England and France. In his respect for the Spanish heritage, his ideas corresponded to those guiding the government of President Rafael Carrera in neighboring Guatemala at the same time. Alamán held there were two distinct movements favoring Mexican independence, the first initiated in 1810 by Miguel Hidalgo whom Alamán deprecated, and the second, which effected independence in 1821 under the leadership of Augustín de Iturbide. Independence constituted a political break with Spain unrelated to the plebian uprising of 1810. Iturbide emerged the hero; Hidalgo, the demagogue. Mora was less specific.

Holding to the Liberal interpretation, he judged the independence movement as integral, initiated by Hidalgo and carried to its ultimate success by Iturbide. Mora's emphasis fell on the achievement of independence, the end of Spanish tyranny, the emergence of the Mexican nation. Historiographical studies dwell on the apparent difference separating Liberal and Conservative interpretations of Mexican history. Still, the similarities seem more significant that the differences. In the final analysis, both concluded that the creoles effected independence and that Mexico was a pseudo-European state linked to the Old World through Spain. Neither considered the input or the interests of the Indian majority. When they considered the Indians it was to brand them a threat to "civilization" (defined, as always, in European terms). In short, both Liberal and Conservative historians advocated a political, economic, and social order based on inherited institutions and creole supremacy. They revered the land structure and labor systems, the hierarchy of privileges.

Fiery historiographical debates might have raged, but their outcome for the Indian, African, mestizo, and mulatto majorities and the inherited institutions was the same. The lively discussions among Clio's disciples in nineteenth-century Latin America concerned details rather than substance. The question was not whether to Europeanize but how, not whether to foster capitalism but how to expedite it. No consideration was given to the reality that a majority had no connection with Europe but rather had their own folk cultures and preferred communal arrangements to "competitive" ones. Given the lifestyles of the elites, the preferences of the historians were logical. They were a vocal element of the elites. It would seem unrealistic to attribute to their historiographical debates much more than class interests. For that reason, the similarities in their discussions were more striking than the differences. The frothy historical debate pitting Bartolomé Mitre against Vicente Fidel López in the early 1880s aptly illustrated the underlying uniformity among historians. The debate seemed to focus on the use of documentation and its interpretation, questions as it turned out more of methodology than of meaning. When the sound and fury of heated charges and countercharges subsided, the two historians shook hands and admitted they were essentially in agreement. López asked, "After all, what have

General Mitre and I disputed? Don't events and the valuable and numerous documents prove and justify our agreement?" Mitre wrote his former opponent that, indeed, basic ideas united them: "Our judgment is more or less the same."

Organically integrated, the historians viewed history as a continuous movement toward the realization of their desired goals, ultimately, of course, the goals of the elites. The historians accepted independence, the new national governments (which is to say, the dominance of the creoles within the familiar institutional framework of the past), and the urge to Europeanize. The ultimate aspiration was Europeanization. The Latin American historians believed Europe to be the focal point of history, regarding their own histories as extensions of European. The Old World provided the impetus; the rest of the world reacted. The Latin Americans inherited such ideas from the Enlightenment, but they were also explicit in Comte's positivism: a master program of social organization displayed in different places characteristics of different stages but all within a single, constant pattern of evolution. To the degree their nations came to resemble Europe in the nineteenth century, the historians judged they had "developed" or "progressed." Consequently the men and movements favoring independence and Europeanization received praise from Clio's pens. The failure to Europeanize or the tardiness of Europeanization required explanation and the obstacles, condemnation. Barros Arana in many ways typified the historical perspective of the century when he concluded that history "permits us to observe in general terms the progressive march of humanity and to appreciate the moral laws on which its development depends." Commentators on Guatemala's past described their nation advancing through stages toward a complex and desirable civilization. They were wont to compare their nation to a person growing from an Indian infancy to the maturity of European-adapted civilization. Mariano Zeceña, in his book on the reforms of the Justo Rufino Barrios period, summed up those ideas in this positivist fashion: "Peoples, like individuals, have the period of childhood, of education and growth, of perfection and also of decadence which precedes death." Such teleological views constantly remind us of the intellectual's heavy debt to the philosophes of the Enlightenment as well as their later — and natural — conversion to the theories of Spencer and Comte.

The exclusivity of Latin American historiography deflected attention from the alternatives to Europeanization even though the majority of the populations still favored and practiced those alternatives. The historiographical treatment of the Americas in which "History" began with the arrival of the Iberian conquerors relegated the long and the rich Indian past to the anthropologists or to those who practiced that discipline's nineteenth-century antecedent. Historians ingored folk cultures (except occasionally to disparage them), and although forced to deal with populist caudillos, they were quick to deprecate them. For example, once the traditional elites returned to power in Buenos Aires in 1852, they not only set about eliminating the populist caudillos in the interior and in neighboring Paraguay but writing history complimentary to their actions, the official textbooks that nurtured succeeding generations of Argentine schoolchildren. Mitre, both a prolific historian and energetic president of the nation, subscribed fully to the elitist concept of Europe as the single source of civilization. He believed that the educated minority made history and should impose its will on the ignorant masses. On the one hand, as president, he opened the doors to foreign penetration and facilitated European economic and cultural domination. On the other, as an historian, he shaped the past to suit his present ends. Leaders with whom he disagreed he simply erased from the pages of history or relegated to inferior or negative positions. He informed fellow historian López, "We have almost the same predilection for great men and the same repulsion for the barbarian troublemakers such as [José Gervasio] Artigas whom we have buried historically." His philosophy recalls the Confucian mandarins who referred to rebels and dissidents as *fei,* a negative grammatical expression meaning a nonperson, one who is not recognized by history. The task of disinterring what previous generations of historians have buried is not an easy one, and it is complicated by the fact that most of society never articulated in written form its complaints, alternatives, or activities.

A basic ideological conformity characterized the Latin American historians during much of the nineteenth century.

Probably their most important ideological commitment was to "progress," which they equated with Europeanization. By ignoring those aspects and sectors of their society that resisted the European siren, the historians omitted the majority of the populations from their pages. When they did notice the masses in their accounts, it was generally to deplore them as "backward" and often to advocate immigration to either "civilize" or replace them. Their heavy reliance on European historical thought and methodologies blurred their vision of their own national past. European approved or inspired themes — the Romantics' search for the noble Indian, the Spencerian attraction to social evolution, or the positivist concern with political order and material progress — received their preference. Besides stunting the historians' own intellectual growth, the overdose of intellectual derivation condemned Latin America psychologically to an inferior position. The historians inevitably compared their own nations to Northern Europe and the United States. By masochistically insisting on judging themselves by the experiences and conditions of others, the historians separated their own societies from their context and not surprisingly found them wanting. Few were perceptive or critical enough to realize that the Europeanization they approved contributed to their nation's dependency. Few appreciated the geographical, racial, and historical uniqueness of Latin America.

While these conclusions may hold few surprises, the implications that might be drawn from this narrow historiographical base deserve attention. Most thought-provoking is the realization that the consistency and frequency of the themes emphasized by the majority of the nineteenth-century historians created an "ideology of class." That ideology rationalized the institutions and the elites who controlled them, a justification that helped legitimize both and contributed to their continuity. The values and goals of that ideology served the elites well as one effective means to coerce larger and larger segments of the population into accepting the institutional structures and social systems of Latin America in the past century, even though those structures and systems were more detrimental than beneficial to an overwhelming majority of the population. The historians contributed mightily to the creation of a sense and feeling of nationality, albeit one complimentary to the interests of the elites. In doing so, they successfully shrouded national histories with a sacred mystique, which has inhibited broader historical investigations and even ridiculed the posing of some fundamental historical questions that might cast doubt on the efficacy of "modernization," "progress," "development," not to mention the national institutions themselves.

Indeed, nineteenth-century historians set patterns and emphasized preferences that to an astonishing degree still pervade twentieth-century historiography. Sarmiento's *Civilización y Barbarie,* a paean to Europe and a denigration of Argentina, is still dutifully read by Argentine schoolchildren. The implication remains that what is foreign is superior to what is indigenous. For that matter, Vicente Fidel López's *Compendio de Historia Argentina, Adaptado a la Enseñanza de los Colegios Nacionales,* published in two volumes, 1889–1890, with its emphasis on Europeanization and the political activities of the elites of Buenos Aires, continued to be used by Argentine school teachers at least through the 1930s; thus, like Sarmiento's work, a bridge for the ideas of nineteenth-century historiography to cross into the present. Early in the twentieth century, two Brazilian historians, José Francisco da Rocha Pombo and João Ribeiro, wrote popular histories of their country synthesizing much of the material written in the last half of the nineteenth century. Both texts have gone through repeated reprints until the present day and have been read by generations of secondary school students. The texts offer a view of Brazil restricted by a class perspective of the last century. For example, both hardly mention the blacks, even though they constituted a majority of the population for centuries and made monumental contributions to Brazil. In a text of 493 pages (the tenth edition), Rocha Pombo spoke directly of them on only seventeen, most of which concerned the slave trade and the abolition movement. Ribeiro did much the same on sixteen out of 423 pages (the seventeenth edition). A Brazilian history text, *História do Brasil,* published in 1961 by Hélio Vianna and widely used in university courses, altered not one whit the emphasis of Rocha Pombo and Ribeiro. Serving as a sobering example of historiographical continuity, it devoted only twenty-one out of 671 pages to the African background of

Brazil and the blacks' experience in Brazil. Even though written a half century after Rocha Pombo and Ribeiro, the Vianna text still emphasizes the slave trade and abolition to the exclusion of myriad other black themes. The cult of the national hero continues to be well tended by the high priests of Clio in the twentieth century, and it is tempting to broaden that observation to conclude that the "great man" theory of history persists.

In viewing nineteenth-century Latin America, historians as a group still seem to subscribe to the fundamental tenet of the historiography of that century: modernization and consequently Europeanization were desirable, and conversely traditional folk cultures were detrimental. This indoctrination handed down by the nineteenth-century historians is so effective that few will concede that the modernization that took place in Latin America actually deepened dependency and lowered the quality of life of the majority. Accepting the conclusion that folk cultures were "backward," historians therefore did not question whether they might have provided the majority with a more satisfactory life-style. Historiography served the elites well through its selectivity of themes, its praise of Europeanization, and its neglect of the alternative preferences. Those alternatives merit more attention than they have received.

CHAPTER FOUR

An Intellectual Counterpoint

Not all the elites subscribed to the idea of unmediated modernization. The implications inherent in the commitment to Europeanize Latin America provoked some questioning and criticism, particularly from some patriarchs and intellectuals. A few intellectuals recognized the masquerade in which Latin America's progress dressed. Some greatly satirized the situation. With less a sense of humor, others raged about the injustices inflicted. An even greater number began to perceive problems in the new societies, problems they could identify and denounce but of whose roots and causes they seemed less certain. With the aid of hindsight perhaps we can trace those problems at least partly to the form of progress in vogue.

By midcentury, if not sooner, those intellectuals began to voice second thoughts about the impact and forms of progress. Disgusted with the slavish aping of Northern Europe and the United States, they cautioned that any Westernization should proceed slowly, mediated with Iberian and American values. While ably advocating and defending their ideas, those intellectuals failed to retard the momentum or alter the thrust of modernization. Because they failed to stem the trend, the tendency has been to neglect their ideas and their significance or, in the case of a few intellectual giants, to focus attention on the more conventional aspects of their writing while overlooking the more novel. Juan Bautista Alberdi, for example, has been quoted much more extensively from his early writings as an adherent to the ideas of the Generation of 1837 than from the later ones critical of that movement.

The insights pervading the criticism of those intellectuals are invaluable in the reconstruction of a fuller understanding of the nineteenth century. Further their ideas also merit consideration since they constitute possible solutions to problems Latin America confronted in the past century and in most cases still faces in the twentieth. They indicated roads that might have been followed — indeed, in some cases, could still be followed — to reach the goal of national development; or perhaps it is better to understate it and say national well-being. What is more, their ideas assume significance as an expression of political, cultural, and/or economic nationalism, a force to be reckoned with in the twentieth century.

A growing realization that political independence had brought few meaningful changes to Latin America while, in fact, strengthening some of the most iniquitous institutions, the rural structures for example, prompted an increasing number of the intellectuals to avert their eyes from Europe and to investigate national reality. They began to perceive that the brand of "progress' their governments encouraged was at best cosmetic and at worst another bond further tightening their subordination to Europe. Arrogant European ethnocentricity stung their pride, prompting some of them to sharpen their defense of local culture. Their challenge to European solutions posed more questions that it answered, and the dissenters spent the century wrestling with some of the dilemmas. This chapter will introduce some of those dissenters and their contributions.

The nebulous concept of progress was both an easy and difficult target for the dissenters. It was easy because few of its proponents had bothered to define it and, when they had, they relied too much on the European experience to give it much meaning for the New World. It was difficult because the critical intellectuals were vague or hesitant about alternatives to Eurocentricity.

Fittingly, Alberdi began to question, by the mid-1850s, his peers' concept of progress and the civilization it was supposed to engender in Latin America. Since that generation formulated most impressively Latin America's ideology of progress, Alberdi's criticism of it constitutes the appropriate material with which to begin the questioning. The very loyalty to federalist convictions that had prompted Alberdi to leave the Argentina of Rosas in 1838 precipitated in 1853 his break with Mitre,

Sarmiento, and the Generation of 1837. During the remaining thirty-one years of his life, he criticized the program of the men who advocated the rapid Europeanization of Argentina as the panacea of ills past. His views of Rosas moderated during those years to the point where he lamented his former attacks on the gaucho caudillo. Boldly Alberdi challenged the central premise of the modernizers by denouncing Sarmiento's *Civilización y Barbarie* as invalid. Ridiculing Sarmiento's central thesis, he proclaimed, "Characterizing the cities as civilized and the countryside as barbarian is an error of judgment and history." The urban educated had behaved far more barbarously than the country folk, Alberdi asserted:

> There exists an educated barbarism a thousand times more disastrous for true civilization than that of all the savages of the American hinterlands. . . . The educated barbarians of the city have eclipsed the rural caudillos with their wars twice as long, twice as bloody, twice as costly and disastrous as those of Rosas and Quiroga. Neither of those barbarians contracted loans for sixty millions of hard pesos, allowed the public debt to absorb half the national budget with interest payments, levied taxes higher than those paid in England, or allowed insecurity to reign in the city and countryside alike. . . .

That reversal of the barbarity-civilization dichotomy occurred elsewhere in Latin America, too, although it never gained wide acceptance among the elites. The Bolivian José Maria Dalence wrote at midcentury that many of the Indian groups of his nation exhibited greater intelligence than some Europeans. In a *"Representación"* of 1866, the Indians of Huancané in the Peruvian highlands accused the local authorities of a "barbarism" reminiscent of the atrocities committed by the Spanish conquerors. The following year *El Nacional* in Lima argued that although it was customary to accuse the Indians of being barbarian, the harships and punishments inflicted on the descendants of the Incas by the authorities surpassed any conventional concept of barbarity.

An occasional author gently satirized the pretentious claims of the cities to their monopoly of progress and civilization. In two short stories at midcentury, the Venezuelan Daniel Mendoza created the wry rustic Palmarote, a *llanero* from the province of Guárico, who innocently delivered some penetrating observations on imported and urban progress. In the first, "Un Llanero en la Capital," Palmarote took note of the contradictions in urban life and, despite the arguments of the "doctor," his conversational companion, remained unconvinced of the "advantages" or "benefits" the city offered. He suggested to the doctor that the city depended on the countryside rather than the contrary as his companion alleged. In "Palmarote en Apure," Mendoza put the doctor in the countryside, where he tried to convince Palmarote of the great advantages that would accrue to Venezuelan progress from accelerated European immigration. While the doctor argued that foreigners would bring progress, Palmarote opined they came to Venezuela only to enrich themselves at the country's expense. In the conversations between the "citified doctor" and the llanero, Mendoza exposed the superficiality of much of the "imported civilization" characteristic of the cities and hinted that if any progress were evident, it benefited Europeans rather than Venezuelans.

Palmarote's observations paralleled the attacks of Alberdi on the Sarmiento thesis. Alberdi, too, pointed out that the rural folk had liberated Argentina from Spain and the maligned countryside produced the nation's wealth. He scoffed at the notion that steam, electricity, or any technological advances conferred "civilization" on their users, a much too superficial and material concept of civilization. He chose to define Argentine civilization in other less conventional terms:

> If there is a part of Argentina which by its geographical and natural conditions represents civilization it is that region composed of green, well-watered, flat, and fresh fields on which millions of animals roam. . . . The horse is another instrument and natural symbol of Argentine civilization, as worthy as the river, canal, or railroad. . . . But the horse is a useless machine without a skilled mechanic to operate it, which is to say without the gaucho who in this sense represents civilization in Argentina. . . . Our fields and our farmers cannot be classified as barbaric except in books written by someone who does not know what civilization is.

Alberdi assigned *progress* and *civilization* new meanings, at least novel ones in Latin America. While the Generation of 1837 equated progress with the replication of Europe in the New World, Alberdi believed it meant improving Argentina to meet broad national needs through the use of national resources and means. Progress, thus, could be defined in terms of national resources, interests, and goals rather than with a made-in-Europe formula to be applied locally whether or not it fit, whether or not it benefited the majority. Significantly, Alberdi's conclusions made progress a relative and not an absolute concept.

Indeed, a few adventurous intellectuals suggested the relativity of civilization, scoffing at the propensity to label the unknown or the non-European as barbarous. Such an idea was not particularly American. Adam Ferguson, professor of moral history at the University of Edinburgh, had phrased it well in 1767, "We are generally at a loss to conceive how mankind can subsist under manners and customs extremely different from our own; and we are apt to exaggerate the misery of barbarous times, by an imagination of what we ourselves should suffer in a situation to which we are not accustomed." Echoing that idea a half-century later, the Mexican José Joaquín Fernández concocted an intriguing conversation in his *El Periquillo Sarnieto* (*The Itching Parrot,* 1816) between a New World black and an English official. The white, convinced that only Europe could boast of civilization, heard a defense of human diversity that made all people strangers to the civilizations of others. Condemnations of inferiority sprang from ignorance or misunderstanding, the Mexican author affirmed. He concluded through his black character, "It is a very gross error to deem stupid or savage all those who do not correspond to our way of thinking." Alas, such an intellectual plea for diversity influenced few of the Latin American elites.

At another time and place but for similar reasons, Sebastião Ferreira Soares mounted a defense of the Indians of the Amazonean region. Their detractors, he charged in 1860, judged them by standards not applicable to the Amazonean environment and Indian values. Civilization, culture, and progress were subjective terms whose European definitions did not fit North Brazil anymore than Indian judgments of Europe based on their American experiences would have been germane. What mattered was that the Amazonean Indians enjoyed peace, quiet, and abundance to a degree that satisfied their desires; in fact, to a degree, Ferreira Soares conjectured, which the European had never achieved. In that perceptive discussion Ferreira Soares touched on the essential topic of relative or subjective progress, which he realized could be considered only in relation to each group's needs. No golden age imagined by the Europeans could be more satisfactory to the Amazonean Indians than the lifestyle they themselves desired, a conclusion difficult if not impossible for the ethnocentric Europeans and their New World enthusiasts to understand and to accept.

The idea was taken up earnestly again by the Cuban patriot-philosopher José Martí, who warned of the undesirability of trying to import a blueprint for progress. His conception of progress as relative to local conditions, resources, and needs complemented the earlier ideas of Fernández, Ferreira Soares, and Alberdi.

In his appreciation and understanding of the rural masses, Martí also expanded on other ideas expressed by Alberdi. He acknowledged the cities as the "brain" of any nation, but in the countryside beat the national "heart." "Sane and wholesome," the countryfolk produced the food and exports of the hemisphere and thus its wealth. They constituted the fundamental component of the nations, which in the final analysis depended on their contribution. Without the well-being of the rural masses no real progress could be achieved, according to Martí. In his sympathetic, yet realistic, treatment of the rural masses, Martí displayed a rare appreciation of their fundamental contribution to any prosperity Latin American might hope to enjoy.

The haphazard importation of modernization posed some serious dilemmas for the intellectuals who, after all, had expected progress to solve, not exacerbate, problems inherited or created by the new nations. While the urge to Europeanize gained momentum with each passing decade, warnings of the dangers of unselective importation of ideas, artifacts, and technology were sounded, a cacophonous counterpoint to the euphoria of the modernizers. Some pointed to a relationship they perceived between the wholesale importation of progress and foreign domination and exploitation. Editorializing in Recife's *A Voz do Brasil* (October 27, 1847), Inácio Bento de Loiola complained bitterly that independence had benefited foreigners rather than Brazilians. While the nationals became poorer each year, the foreigners invested minimal sums to extract fortunes and in the process exerted a decisive influence over imperial politics. He observed that the "dangerous guests" despised Brazilians at the same time they took advantage of them. His sharp attack of foreign economic control and profit making formed the core of later economic nationalism.

Typical of the cautious dissenters a quarter of a century later was Colonel Alvaro Gabriel Barros, an Argentine military man and intellectual who had had extensive experience administering the bureaucracy of the governing elite. He understood that the unselective importation of European solutions for local problems could result in more harm than good:

> In order to avert or cure the ills produced by the present crisis, we have recourse to and study analogous situations in other nations of the world. Once informed of what was done there with success, we take pleasure in implementing their solutions here, certain they will have similar results. We do not take the opportunity or time to study our own country to verify if the conditions are the same here or if the causes that have given rise to the crisis are similar.

Those remarks evinced a disappointment with those intellectuals who knew far more about distant cultures than about their own national reality. Barros went on to criticize their concept of "progress" as one detrimental to the nation and beneficial to Europe:

> The advantages of the railroad lines, the telegraphic network, the artificial ports, etc., will be real and great when such works respond to the needs of our progress, increased production, and enrichment. To invest in their acquisition huge amounts of capital with guaranteed interest as a means of advancing and enriching ourselves when at the same time we permit terrible and powerful agents actively working to exploit our riches is to ensure prosperity for other nations while acquiescing in our own ruin. They come here to crush us beneath their enormous weight.

Barros clearly did not portray Europe as the salutary force many of the elites envisioned.

Charges of a slightly different but related nature against further importation of European civilization came from the pen of the Venezuelan Ramón Ramírez. While questioning Europe as a useful source for solutions to American problems, he advised greater reliance on local values. While a professor at the University of Caracas, he published a fascinating political analysis, *El Cristianismo y la Libertad, Ensayo sobre la Civilización Americana* (1855). "European civilization spawns materialism to the neglect of the spirit," Ramírez charged. While interested in the inventions pouring out of the Old World, he concluded that material advancement had become an end in itself rather than a means to advance public well-being. That the "democracy" being practiced in the Americas facilitated the rule of the privileged few over the many alarmed him. Because European civilization benefited the minority at the expense of the majority, the Americans must resist temptations to copy Europe, the originator, after all, of the hemisphere's present problems, and create a new civilization of their own. Perhaps, he reasoned, the turmoil characteristic of Latin America since independence was the violent gestation of that new civilization. Not immune from European influences himself, Ramírez argued that the new American civilization should be based on the Christian socialism he discussed at length in the second half of his book. All in all, he provided a useful analysis of the New World and suggested a well-argued alternative to the blind copying of Europe in vogue in Venezuela as in other parts of Latin America. Exemplifying a nascent challenge to formerly unquestioned European dicta, Ramírez, like Alberdi, Loiola, Barros, and Martí, revealed a growing preoccupation among the intellectuals with local socioeconomic reality.

Accelerating foreign domination and exploitation with the consequent debilitation of Latin America seemed to some intellectuals too high a price to pay for superficial progress. To those who kept their sense of humor, the cosmetic nature of the imported progress readily lent itself to caricature, and some Latin American writers relished ridiculing their compatriots' blind allegiance to European novelties. Perhaps the master satire came from the pen of the Venezuelan Tulio Febres Cordero, whose amusing novel *Don Quijote en América* (1905) introduced Dr. Quix of Manchester, supposedly the reincarnation of Don Quixote de la Mancha. Dr. Quix arrived in Venezuela dressed like a caricature of the Englishman in the tropics complete with pith helmet and bicycle. He proclaimed his mission to introduce progress, and the natives seemed delighted with the prospects and flattered with the attention. Although no one seemed either to note or to care, the progress introduced was superficial in the extreme, often no more than a change of nomenclature, substituting the pretentious for the simple. Cordero mused, "The sacred law of progress demands daily changes and reforms of objects and their names, no less than of ideas and plans because this continual series of changes is the ocean in which the redeeming ship of civilization floats." Like it or not, the author affirmed, the acquisition of civilization required the abandonment of one's natural tastes, desires, and inclinations for those sanctioned by Europe. In Mapiche, a rustic hamlet where Dr. Quix settled for a brief visit, the old inn, rarely frequented by a guest, became the "Hotel Cosmopolita" and acquired a hand-powered elevator even though it was only a two-story building. Raised from innkeeper to "hotelier," the owner proudly printed the daily menu in English. The local citizenry rejoiced in those and other indubitable manifestations of progress.

Cordero occasionally abandoned satire to muse. Obviously addressing a subject that disturbed him, he observed:

> Opposing progress has come to be a more heinous crime than being unpatriotic because the adjective *progressive* has assumed greater importance than patriotism. For that reason, anything native, anything purely our own, anything that by tradition and nature serves as the basis for our national character, whether in ideas or customs, gives way to the exotic and foreign. In our private as well as public lives, there appears an artificiality and phoniness that we unhesitatingly label civilization and progress when the true name is something quite different because what is happening is nothing less than a carnival game, a showy costume parade of foreign dress, in which we try to hide our indigenous features, ashamed of appearing before the world with our distinctive originality of race, type, ideas, and customs. We forget that originality is one of the primary ingredients for greatness and beauty, that civilization, considered with respect to each people, ought to be like a tree, which grows, matures, and bears fruit from its own seed and nourishment. In that sense, all outside strength, no matter how powerful, has to submit and adapt to the vital primary and indigenous strength. The psychological development of a people and its useful and transcendental progress are not improvised but come logically and gradually. Real progress starts by conserving all that is good, no matter how ancient, and proceeds with the improvement of the existing and the opportune implantation of the new when that novelty is advantageous.

As this statement illustrates, the fictional and satirical setting for Cordero's musng could not disguise his seriousness of purpose. He shared with others first an annoyance with the superficiality of progress and second a suspicion of the increasing insidiousness of the progress mesmerizing most of the elites and the sympathetic middle class.

The questioning of progress accompanied a growing concern among some of the literati with the common people. Occasional writers linked the plight of the people with the accelerating importation of progress. Greater attention to the folk sometimes took the form of *costumbrismo,* which appeared in a variety of literary forms — short stories, sketches, as parts of novels — all of which preserved valuable details of day-to-day life, a kind of verbal snapshot of ordinary people going about their daily tasks. In each country *costumbristas* recorded aspects of national reality, but the acknowledged master was Ricardo Palma, who left a rich legacy of insight into the daily life of both colonial and nineteenth-century Peru.

Gaucho-inspired literature, a genre inspired by the folk tales and poems popular among the peoples of the pampas, further illustrated that concern with common people. It recognized the importance and legitimacy of local sources, vocabulary, themes, and style for literature. In 1872, José Hernández, long an astute social critic, published the first part of his magnificent epic poem *Martín Fierro* (the second came out in 1879). Bristling with sharp social protest, the verses exalted the gaucho whose nobility contrasted sharply with the villainy of the urban politician. Fierro despaired of any relief coming from the cities for the misery of the gaucho. Even those who sympathized with his plight refused to treat the real causes of his problems; Fierro suggested that hypocrisy in this manner:

> The wrongs we suffer
> Make city folks talk a lot,
> But they're like *tero* birds
> Who try to hide their nests:
> They make noises in one place
> And have their eggs someplace else.
>
> And they pretend they can't
> Get to the bottom of the problem;

> While the gaucho is hounded
> Without mercy by the law.
> They keep the disease
> As far as they can from the cure.

The city was at best indifferent, at worst destructive; the purity of the countryside had been polluted; injustice masqueraded as civilization. The poem sounded the call for a new caudillo to save the people:

> For me, the tail is tenderloin
> And the spine is filet,
> I'll make my nest wherever I am
> And eat whatever I find;
> I'll go around meek as a lamb
> And knock on any door.
>
> And I'll let the ball roll on,
> Since some day it's got to stop;
> A gaucho has to put up with things,
> Until that hole in the ground swallows him up,
> Or until some real man comes along
> To take over out here.

Lack of such leadership doomed indigenous Argentina to be Europeanized and condemned the folk to abandon their own style of living. The poem related an epic battle, the folk and their culture struggling against the elites and European civilization to determine the destiny of Argentina. While the Argentine literary establishment dismissed the poem, it enjoyed unprecedented popular success, going through edition after edition of thousands of copies each. The people obviously read in the poem a truth, a vindication that appealed to them. They identified with it, something they were unable to do with the standard Europeanized literature of the elite.

Eduardo Gutierrez picked up the gaucho themes for his novel *Juan Moreira,* first serialized in the newspaper in 1879–80. The plot depicted the hardworking gaucho as a victim of an unjust society. In 1886, the novel was dramatized in a circus pantomime to enthusiastic public acclam. Drama historians consider its production as the origin of the national theater.

Finally, in Rafael Obligado's allegorical poem *Santos Vega* (1887), the death knell for the gaucho sounded. The *payador*

Santos Vega encountered the devil in the person of Juan Sin Ropa in the peom's climactic scene. Vega, embodying the gauchos, and Sin Ropa, the Circe of progress, engaged in a Homeric song contest. Sin Ropa issued the irresistible call of progress and triumphed. Brokenhearted, Santos Vega died. Romanticism might have tinted the intellectuals' coloration of the countryside, but it did not always blur the realities.

In Brazil, as elsewhere, some intellectuals in their examination of national reality sought local and popular roots for national culture. The crises shaking the once somnolent empire after 1865 prompted the intellectual inquiry. A new bourgeoisie taking shape as the cities grew in size felt strong enough to challenge the old rural oligarchy for power. The expensive and protracted war with Paraguay, 1864–70, the rise of republican sentiment, and abolitionist campaigns that challenged the hoary institution of slavery excited debate and precipitated the rise and fall of several governments. Those crises stimulated literary production and were in turn aggravated by social criticism from the literati who increasingly occupied themselves with questions of national self-examination.

Sílvio Romero, one of the most skilled analyst of Brazil, wrote prolifically, but no work exceeds in importance his monumental *História da Literatura Brasileira* (1888). Of lasting value, it remains as essential today for an understanding of Brazil as it was when first published. Romero considered literature as a national expression, an integral part of society, an inescapable conclusion in Brazil where the literati played multiple roles in society. He lamented that Brazilian literature and history had placed excessive emphasis on the elite to the neglect of the people, whom he considered the basic force of society. In efforts to relate the masses and literature, he published two anthologies of folk poems and songs: *Contos Populares do Brasil* (1885) and *Estudos sôbre a Poesia Popular do Brasil* (1888). Although he had to deal with European racist doctrine, which influenced and would continue to influence so many Brazilian intellectuals, he boldly proclaimed that Brazil was not the exclusive product of Europe but the joint effort of Indians, Europeans, and Africans, a truly revolutionary thesis at the time. He was the first Brazilian intellectual to accord the blacks their just position alongside the other races in the construction of Brazil. He lauded miscegenation, which he concluded would guarantee a vigorous new race, the core of Brazil. The mestizo was Brazil's hope, and the thorough mixture of all races differentiated Brazil from other countries. Romero introduced a host of popular topics, which would be explored by later nationalists and scholars.

Advocating national introspection, Romero aimed his critical barbs at "the figure of the imitator, of the slavish and witless copier of each and every trifle that the ships from Portugal or France or any other place bring us." He crusaded for a Brazilian literature with its roots in the people, one which would interpret the national environment, traditions, and sentiments. The major obstacle to such national expression, he concluded, was that "we do not know ourselves."

Between 1884 and 1904, Alexandre José de Melo Moraes Filho published a long series of books and essays on the popular customs in Brazil. Although he lacked the perception of Romero, his compilations provided valuable material for future scholars and also revealed a new effort on the part of the intellectuals to draw on local sources rather than rely on Europe for inspiration.

Those intellectuals searching for local inspiration and American originality logically returned to the theme of the Indian, after all the original inhabitant. Just as inevitably that group of intellectuals regarded the Indian as "the noble savage," a theme not always in vogue but one that could easily be traced to late fifteenth-century roots. Their romanticization of the Indian was easy to discern, just as the reasons for it were easy to explain. Yet beneath the superficiality of treatment, a defiant voice arose from the intellectuals recognizing and denouncing the injustice perpetuated on the native race and by inference on the Americas. They were quick to point out the Indians' contributions to national formation and the unique and positive values of their civilizations.

Some notable literati effectively denounced the abuses inflicted on the Indians. Clorinda Matto de Turner, discussed in chapter two, ably represented that group. Yet, others went on to acknowledge the Indians' harmony with their environment, by implication a contrast with the conflicts, the natural versus the artificial, engendered by wholesale importation of European civilization into the New World. In his *O Indio Afonso* (1873), the Brazilian novelist Bernardo Guimarães created an extraordinary native protagonist who was one with nature, believed by some whites to be the son of an Indian and the devil of waters (in itself a revealing indication of how the whites regarded nature). Afonso survived the violence and persecution of the police, the symbol of the Europeanized state, because he understood and used his environment. He knew how to navigate the rivers and to hide in the forest, while both hindered the advance and effectiveness of the police. José de Alencar, one of the major Brazilian novelists of the last century, had hoped to be freed from the "ideas of civilized men" so that he could praise and appreciate the unequaled natural beauty of Brazil. His novels, too, depicted the close relationship of the Indians with their environment.

The Indians' harmony with their environment meant they had much to teach the European immigrants about the utilization of the land, its rivers, and their products, among other things. They bequeathed a formidable legacy to the new nations, often forgotten, neglected, or disparaged by an elite determined to Europeanize their nations. Juan E. O'Leary paid eloquent tribute to the contributions of the Guaraní to Paraguay in a poem he ironically entitled "Salvaje" (1902). He acknowledged:

> You have given everything:
> Your beautiful land,
> Your passionate blood,
> Your fearless courage,
> Your sublime and incomparable unselfishness,
> Your melodious language.

Generally those contributions went unrewarded, even unappreciated in the rush toward Europeanization.

In some rare instances the Latin American intellectuals moved beyond the literary defense of the Indians to the physical. Juan Bustamante of Peru provides an excellent, if rare, example of commitment and activism. An unusual combination of merchant, reformer, political activist, and intellectual, Bustamente operated a wool business in the altiplano near Puno. In the 1850s, he had served as a deputy in the national congress, been the prefect of Huancavelica, and traveled in Europe. In the early 1860s he wrote a defense of the Indians, published in 1867 in *Los Indios del Peru*. The same year he

founded the Society of the Friends of the Indians. The altiplano merchant-intellectual by no means acted alone in his
support of the Indians. As his book reveals, his efforts found an
echo among some intellectuals in the capital, and some of the
national press commended the Soceity. In the Indian uprising
of 1867, Bustamente assumed a leadership role. The Indians
seized Puno and threatened Cuzco. In the process, Bustamente
was taken prisoner by the army and stoned to death. The living
conditions of the highland Indians appalled the wool merchant, who daily had occasion to observe them. He understood
that the future of Peru depended on the Indians' well-being.
His plan was revolutionary only in that he wanted to put into
practice long-recognized, but ignored legal rights: to extend to
the Indians the protections of life and property guaranteed by
the constitution but enjoyed exclusively by the landowning
elite. Of course in practice such protection for the Indians
would have altered profoundly national life. Declaring, "The
Indian is inferior to no person," Bustamente predicted a prom-
ising future for the Indians and for Peru if they were allowed to
keep and work their lands, to enjoy the same liberties monopolized by the elites, and to cultivate their intelligence. In short,
he believed in the logical extension to all peoples of the rights
generated by the Enlightenment. He died defending those beliefs, an extremely rare martyr among the merchant class — and
among intellectuals, too, for that matter.

The favorable attention these intellectuals focused on the
Indians, as well as on the gaucho and other representatives of
the popular classes, drew into the discussions considerations of
both folk cultures and folk societies. Focusing on those topics, it
was inevitable that the intellectuals would concern themselves
with questions involving the land, not only an appreciation of
the splendid diversity and beauty of nature but of the practical
and essential problems of land ownership and use.

Latin America's most precious resource was its soil, and so
long as agrarian mismanagement continued, the economic
conditions of the nations and the life-styles of the rural masses — the majority of the population — remained miserable in the
nineteenth century. Land concentration in the hands of a few
rural landlords accelerated rapidly. They expanded their estates
partly to increase production of profitable agrarian exports

—sugar, coffee, wheat, tobacco, beef, wool, cacao—but equally to speculate and to ensure a ready rural labor supply, accomplished largely by depriving the Indians and peasants of their lands, although the wealthy benefited handsomely through the state confiscation and sale of church and crown lands as well. Huge estates were only partially and inefficiently worked. Yet, there was little land for those who wanted to work. One inevitable result of agrarian mismanagement was the increase in the price of basic foodstuffs. In 1856, the leading newspaper of Brazil's vast Northeast, *Diário de Pernambuco,* reminded its readers of the importance of agriculture not only as the present source of income but also as the future hope of development. It concluded that a "barrier" prevented the full exploitation of the agrarian potential:

> And what is that barrier? Large landholdings. It is the terrible curse that has ruined and depopulated many other nations.
> This region that extends along the entire coast of our province and inland for ten, twelve, or, at times, fifteen and eighteen leagues is divided into sugar plantations and properties whose dimensions vary from a quarter of a league square to two and three and even four and five leagues square. . . . But still a major part of the plantations possesses vast extensions of uncultivated land that would be especially well suited for the small farmer and which, if cultivated, would be sufficient to furnish abundantly flour, corn, beans, etc., to all the population of the province and of the neighboring provinces with some produce left over for exportation.

At the same time in Rio de Janeiro, amid a region undergoing a heady boom in coffee production, Sebastião Ferreiro Soares came to similar conclusions about the distortion of the economy through land misuse and export orientation. He observed with alarm the rapid extension of the export sector accompanied by declining production of food for internal consumption, a trend he documented with convincing statistical evidence. He noted that foods exported from Rio de Janeiro as late as 1850 were being imported a decade later. Prices of basic foodstuffs—beans, corn, flour—rose accordingly. By withholding most of their acreage from cultivation, the large landowners caused the spiraling costs of foodstuffs, deprived the rural inhabitants of steady employment, and consequently encouraged the unemployed or underemployed to migrate to the cities where no jobs awaited them. A few became wealthy from the export of coffee, while the majority suffered loss of land and employment with the resultant misery. In short, the emphasis on export crops abused the land to the detriment of the majority of the population. These trends observed in Brazil by midcentury were evident throughout much of Latin America where the dynamic sector of the rural economies was export-oriented, coupling the Latin American economies with those of the North Atlantic, reducing land options, and further impoverishing the masses.

Some who perceived the problems resulting from the mismanagement and overconcentration of the arable lands in the hands of fewer and fewer owners advocated land reform. They spoke mainly, but not exclusively, of redistributing uncultivated lands. In their discussions, they addressed the basic cause of Latin America's plight, for more than anything else land misuse contributed to the enigma of poverty amid potential plenty.

During the early stages of the Mexican independence struggle, Miguel Hidalgo and José María Morelos advocated profound agrarian reforms. In Uruguay, the caudillo José G. Artigas decreed some far-reaching changes in land structure and use in 1815, only to be thwarted in executing them by the Portuguese invasion of his homeland. In Mexico shortly after independence, Francisco Severo Maldonado warned of the dangers of concentration of land in the hands of a few. National prosperity, he believed, depended on widespread ownership of land, and he advocated the establishment of a bank to buy land from those who owned large, unused parcels and to sell it "at the lowest possible price" to those who have no land. By 1860 Ferreira Soares of Brazil was advocating that uncultivated land be put in the hands of people who would work it. Decades later, Sílvio Romero indicated he had a vision of the Brazilian future as well as its past. He understood that before Brazil could develop, it would be necessary to reform basic agrarian institutions by abolishing slavery and redistributing the land. Such reforms would be essential, he concluded, if Brazil were really to modernize and/or to develop. In the Argentine press, José Hernández also campaigned for agrarian reforms. An editorial in the Buenos Aires newspaper *El Río de la Plata,* September 1, 1869, lamented, "The huge fortunes have the alarming tendency to grow even larger, and their owners possess vast tracts of land, which lie fallow and abandoned. Their greed for land exceeds their ability to use it intelligently and actively." After the turn of the century, a group of articulate Peruvian intellectuals, Manuel González Prada, José A. Encinas, and José Carlos Mariátegui, among others, rated a reform of the land structures to benefit the Indians as the first and most basic step toward national development. Mariátegui succinctly summarized their position in the mid-1920s:

> The problem of the Indian is rooted in the land tenure system of our economy. Any attempt to solve it with administrative or police measures, through education or a road-building program, is superficial and secondary as long as the feudalism of the *gamonales* continues to exist.

Meanwhile Mexico had taken the first faltering steps toward land reform.

The critical assessment of contemporary society extended into historiography during the last decades of the century. Larger urban populations, a growing middle class, and more complex manifestations of nationalism prompted shifts in historical perspectives. Ironically, but predictably, European concerns with "scientific" history and greater "objectivity" echoed in the Western Hemisphere, helping to initiate a questioning of documents and accepted interpretations, and contributing to the more nationalistic tendencies in historiography. While shifting the emphasis from exclusive European input, the revisionists broadened the scope of national history to chronicle the participation of a wider variety of groups. In their challenge to the conventional elitist historiography, the innovators suggested some useful themes, which later generations explored more fully.

In Argentina, the standard interpretations of Bartolomé Mitre, Vicente Fidel López, and Domingo Faustino Sarmiento, who had lauded foreign influence and discredited the aspirations of the people outside of Buenos Aires, fell under scrutiny. The major historical controversy that followed centered on the figure of the caudillo Juan Manuel de Rosas who, during more than two decades of power, had defied the Europeans, withstood French and English blocades, held a tight reign on the local elite, and enjoyed a genuine popularity among the masses. When Adolfo Saldías published his three-volume *Historia de Rosas y su Epoca* (1881, 1884, 1887) and Ernesto Quesada his *La Epoca de Rosas* (1898), they brought into question some of the elitist prejudices that had clouded the perspective of generations of historians who routinely damned Rosas conceding only that he had been the most powerful and successful of the "barbaric" caudillos. Quesada, who had been able to interview Rosas in England, pointed to some positive contributions of Rosas: national unity and stability—achievements that the elites could only prize and the positivists praise. According to Quesada, the progress of Argentina in the last half of the century was possible only because of the firm national foundation Rosas laid. Such new studies suggested a reconsideration of the past that would assign Rosas a key nationalistic role. Those historians set in motion a heated debate, which still rages over the significance of Rosas in Argentine history. Some of the most recent revisionists' examinations of nineteenth-century Argentina conclude that genuine national development took place during the Rosas years, while deepening dependency characterized the nation's fate during the remaining half-century.

Meanwhile, José María Ramos Mejía introduced into Argentine historiography some aspects of the positivist theories of psychology. In his *Las Neurosis de los Hombres Celebres en la Historia Argentina* (2 vols., 1878 and 1888), he attempted to psychoanalyze such prominent historical figures as Juan Manuel de Rosas and José Gaspar Rodrígues de Francia. In later works, *La Locura en la Historia* (1895), *Las Multitudes Argentinas* (1899), and *Rosas y su Tiempo* (1907), the physician-historian turned his attention from individuals to attempt a psychoanalysis of the Argentine masses. Unique contributions, those studies of collective psychology viewed the "great men" as the instruments of larger segments of the population, quite a contrast with the usual conclusions of the period. Rosas emerged from Ramos Mejía's studies as both the product of Argentine society of the first half of the century and personification of that period. His psychological and sociological analyses were significant contributions in nineteenth-century historiography.

In Brazil during the last quarter of the century, João Capistrano de Abreu denounced his compatriots' propensity to ape European trends and lamented that in its imitation of the Old World, Brazilian culture did not represent the "conscious expression of the people." He revolutionized historical studies in Brazil by turning attention from the coastal band with its obvious link to Europe and by examining the previously little known interior. He presented his major thesis in 1889 in a short, but brilliant essay, *Os Caminhos Antigos e o Povoamento do Brasil,* the single most important statement on Brazilian history yet made. Neglecting the archbishops, generals, and viceroys who had populated histories of Brazil to that date — even refusing to treat the official national hero, Tiradentes, whom he considered more the creation of the elite than a representative of the Brazilian people — he concentrated on the contributions of the masses, meaningful periodization of the past, and significant themes. He wrote:

> In history we only point to the dominant figures, those who destroyed or constructed, leaving behind a trail of blood or a ray of hope. We do not remember the shoulders that bore them, or the courage of the masses that gave them their strength, the collective mind that exalted their minds, the unknown hands that pointed out to them the ideal that only the most fortunate attained. And often the unknown person is the one whose cooperation was most vital in bringing about the great event.

If the masses made history, it was the interior, which constituted the true Brazil, the valid national reality. Only when the coastal inhabitants turned their backs on the sea and penetrated the interior did they shed their European ways and become Brazilianized. His *Caminhos Antigos* contained a remarkable global vision of the Brazilian past, which emphasized the themes of exploration and settlement of the interior, the creation of overland and fluvial transportation networks to weld the vast nation together, and the psychological changes of the Brazilian people over the centuries. Capistrano de Abreu focused attention on the national heartland and the people who opened and settled it.

Fascinating as were Capistrano de Abreu, Quesada, and Ramos Mejía (as well as others who could augment the ranks of the innovators), it must be reemphasized that they were not typical of the historiography of their century. Probably they intrigue us because they stand out as precursors of twentieth-century concern and thus more in harmony with later historians than with their own contemporaries. These innovators represent a small, though significant, group of historians who questioned standard interpretations and in the process emphasized New World themes rather than the links with Europe.

The debates of the intellectuals are easy to follow since the published views of the participants are still readily available. Their discussions, although emotional at times, were more often than not carried on pacifically in the fashion of a formalized debating society. An increasing number questioned the blind acceptance of Northern European ideas, values, and technology as progress. The foreign domination and exploitation that inevitably accompanied the adoption of that progress angered them. They also deepened their insight into their own societies beset with dilemmas and devoted some attention to the common people and their problems, most notably the iniquitous land structure. The views of some dissenters were offered in this chapter to indicate philosophical divisions among the elites themselves as well as to introduce some of the differing ideas, but it must be reemphasized that those dissidents constituted a minority whose effectiveness time and space reduced.

CHAPTER FIVE

The Patriarchal Preference

While Latin America in the nineteenth century provides many examples of landowners eager to modernize their farming methods and thus to gain advantages in the international markets, it also offers evidence of other, more cautious and traditional landowners, particularly the patriarchs. The patriarchal estate had acquired a "way of life" of its own, conscious, definite, and coherent. While partly derivitive of European practice, that ethos owed much of its vigor to the American environment and experience. To modernize meant a conscious conversion from the "American way" to the "European way" with an inevitable change of values. Not all the patriarchs welcomed the changes inherent in modernization. To many, modernization implied a threat to their estates whose neofeudalistic character blunted the penetration of capitalism. Understanding the challenge to their way of life, the rural patriarchs reacted accordingly. Their rationale and strength served, at least for a time, as bulwarks against modernization.

For centuries the rural patriarchs had dominated much of Latin America. They controlled vast acreages of land almost as if they were principalities. In addition to the fields for growing the commercial crops as well as subsistence crops, the estates often included orchards, pastures for pack animals, cattle, sheep, and goats, and forests for firewood. Still, most of the estates lay unused. Self-contained as much as possible, they counted on their own carpenters, smithies, bakers, seamstreses, candle and soap makers, and a host of skilled and semiskilled workers to satsify nearly all the simple, local demands. The estates were a way of life, a society unto themselves. Scant need existed for contact with the world beyond the estates' boundaries. Most of the workers were born, reared, and died right on the estates. Only a few of them on infrequent occasions ever left that self-contained, rural world.

The landlord, a patriarchal chief, ruled family, servants, slaves, tenant farmers, sharecroppers, peasants, and even neighbors — unless they happened to be large-estate owners like himself — with absolute authority. The vastness of the estate, its isolation from the seat of government, the relative weakness of local bureaucrats, and the propensity of the government to side with the landed class, all strengthened his power. Furthermore, the estate chaplain and local parish priest orbited around him like satellites, lending the prestige of the Catholic Church to augment his authority. The identification of God with patriarch provided a potent rationale for the rural realities.

From the comfort and security of his house, because naturally the "big house" was the nucleus of the estate's activity, the patriarch administered his holdings, conducted his business, listened to petitions from his subordinates, dispensed justice, and in general held court. These large, strong, but rather simply furnished houses sat in the midst of barns, stables, carriage houses, warehouses, workshops, granaries, and a chapel. In the lowland plantations, the slave quarters stood nearby; in the highlands the Indian peons often lived in villages on the estates. The paterfamilias and other males of the household liberally expanded the basic family unit through their polygamous activities to include hosts of mestizo and mulatto children. In fact, in and around the "big house" European, Indian, and African cultures blended together to create a unique indigenous one. The patriarchs professed a dual loyalty to their Iberian roots and New World environment, cultural as well as geographical. The traditional godparent relationship further ramified and reinforced the family structure. Certain ideal modes were set for the behavior of the women of the patriarch's family, who were destined for either marriage or the religious orders. Virgins until their marriages, they lived separated as much as possible even after matrimony from all men except their fathers, uncles, husbands, and sons. A high value was placed on their duties as wives and mothers. Women of other economic strata could not follow this elitist model, but they certainly were influenced by it. Profoundly Christian and emphatically patriarchal, the families of the large landowners set the social tone and pattern for rural Latin America and for a long time impressed their influence on the urban area as well.

The contacts between the self-contained patriarchal estates and the outside world traditionally had been few. A rough road, probably impassable during the rainy season, led to the next estate and nearest village. From time to time itinerant merchants appeared to peddle their wares. A few crops from the estates sold in local or regional markets, and some were dispatched to the nearest port for export. The patriarchs and part of their families sometimes visited the nearest town or the nation's capital to purchase a few luxury items for themselves and to savor the conviviality and pleasures of urban life. The wealthiest landlords maintained city homes. Often they or a member of their families served in the local municipal government and some also entered the national government.

Incursions into the traditional, isolated, and patriarchal countryside increased after independence. Improved communications, urban growth, and expanding commerce ranked as three powerful catalysts of change in reshaping rural Latin America. Their impact multiplied after midcentury.

First the improvement of roads and ports and then steam power used both for navigation and railroads linked the countryside to the cities more tightly and facilitated integration into European markets. By 1839 a steamship line connected Rio de Janeiro with the northern provinces of the empire, and four years later steam service on the Amazon began. In 1840 the British chartered the Royal Mail Steam Packet Company to provide regular bimonthly service to the entire Caribbean area. The company inaugurated a steam line to Rio de Janeiro in 1851 and to the Rio de la Plata in 1853. The first Latin American railroad began operation in Cuba in 1829; Chile boasted of the second in 1852; Brazil followed with its first line in 1854; Argentina in 1857. On the one hand, the cheaper, quicker, and more efficient transportation helped to speed the raw products from the Latin American countryside to European and North American markets, while on the other it also helped to disseminate new ideas, styles, and technologies from abroad. Another impact on the rural areas was that better communications strengthened the effectiveness of central and provincial governments whose fiat reached out both more quickly and thoroughly to once remote regions, challenging and eventually weakening the once unquestioned authority of the patriarchs.

The improved transportation accelerated the importance of the cities. It facilitated the flow of food and people into urban areas. Increasing numbers of dispossessed or debased rural workers thought they saw in the cities a chance to improve their lot. They contributed to the growth of the cities while at the same time depleting the rural labor supply. The cities hummed as market places and middlemen multiplied to take care of the growing import-export businesses. In the cities decisions were made that increasingly shaped life in the countryside. Banks emerged as powerful institutions that held mortgages on an alarmingly large number of estates. The patriarchs found they had to spend more time in the cities with bankers, agents, and governmental bureaucrats. In the capitals, they had to lobby to protect their interests. Those ever longer periods spent in the cities left an impact if not on the patriarchs, then on their children who came to prefer the bustling urban excitement to the rusticity of the countryside. They quickly adopted the European styles and manners of the urban elite. Ideological lines, which once divided the elites, blurred as the rural patriarchal elite fell under urban influences and control exercised by banks, governmental regulations, marketing realities, and in general the increasingly more aggressive urban elites. Indeed, the sons of that once dominant rural patriarchy passed through the universities to become the doctors, lawyers, engineers, and bureaucrats of the Europeanized sector.

Exports dominated as the dynamic sector of the economy, which in due time challenged and then reduced in number and significance the neofeudal patriarchal estates. Profitable sales abroad meant that commerce played as important, if not more significant, a role as agriculture. The export figures were impressive. While two or three ships a year had handled trade between Chile and England in the 1815-1820 period, more than 300 carried Chilean exports to England in 1847. The value of exports leaving Buenos Aires nearly tripled in a quarter of a century, 1825-50. During the fiscal year 1830-31, Venezuela exported 60,181 bags of coffee, 38,008 bags of cacao, 1,525 head of cattle, and 45,000 hides, which increased in the fiscal year 1847-48 to 200,998 bags of coffee, 66,660 bags of cacao, 15,832 head of cattle, and 365,554 hides. In the last half of the century, the rapid pace of urbanization and industrialization in the United States and Western Europe created an even more frenetic demand for Latin America's raw products. Argentine exports jumped sevenfold between 1853 and 1873 and doubled again by 1893. Argentina made its first wheat shipment to Europe in 1876, a modest 21 tons. By 1900, wheat exports reached 2,250,000 tons. Mexico quadrupled its exports between 1877 and 1900. Between 1833 and 1889, the value of Brazil's foreign trade increased by six to seven times. The smaller nations witnessed proportional increases. Exports of coffee from Costa Rica rose fourfold between 1855 and 1915, while banana exports jumped from 11,000 in 1883 to 10,163,000 in 1914.

While those phenomenal sales provided welcome revenue for national governments and profits for merchants, agents, and landowners, they also wove a tightening web of dependency. The landlords who entered the capitalist marketplace became more closely tied to the cities with their services, capital, and technologies; their welfare rested on the whims of distant marketplaces, which they seldom understood and over which they exercised no control. In their pursuit of profits from distant sales, they changed their agricultural techniques and labor relations: the farm became a factory, the peon a wage laborer.

The landlords who remained more aloof from the capitalist marketplace tried to maintain their patriarchal life-styles, but the major forces at work during the last half of the nineteenth century affected them regardless of their isolation, self-imposed or geographical. Faced with impinging modernization, they chose to minimize or compromise its impact. In doing so, they reaffirmed the Iberian and American values that seemed to them to buttress their life-styles. They did not reject change, although there probably were some among them who wanted to. Rather, they sought to control the change, slowing its pace and modifying its indiscriminate nature. In 1847 the Colombian Rufino Cuervo seemed to sum up the attitude of many of those rural patriarchs favoring the mediation of old and new values: "For a new nation it is as dangerous to innovate totally as it is to maintain everything in a stationary state." The degree of change conceded or mediated by the patriarchs would vary widely from individual to individual, region to region, and according to temporal periods.

Certainly instances existed where the patriarchal reluctance to modernize benefited local folk societies or cultures. Ironically, those patriarchs at times saved the peasants or Indian communities from losing their land and their subsequent absorption into an impersonal labor market. Colombia offers an instructive example of how the patriarchs slowed the capitalist advance into Indian lands. National laws from independence until midcentury facilitated a capitalist absorption of Indians' lands, a process that accelerated more rapidly after midcentury. In the central highlands and immediately contiguous regions, the creole and mestizo elites and foreigners divested the Indians of their lands. However, in the south and southwest, the Indians managed to hang onto their lands until the end of the century. Their survival was due, at least in part, to the patriarchs, principally the powerful ones in the Popayán region, whose distrust of modernization held back the capitalist entrepreneurs and thus protected the Indian communities. Their lands remained relatively safe until the end of the century.

By the late nineteenth century, the Liberals and to a limited extent the Historical Conservatives were well on their way to modernizing Colombia as well as to integrating it into the North Atlantic capitalist system. The Conservatives, by contrast, held back, looking to the patriarchal, Spanish tradition. Despite their initial differences, however, the elites drew together after the Guerra de los Mil Días (the Thousand Days War), 1899–1902. The rising export of coffee created an inevitable alliance to defend and to advance their common interests; and as Charles W. Bergquist also suggests in his *Coffee and Conflict in Colombia, 1886–1910,* all the elites, regardless of political stripe, by then perceived a threat to their rule from the folk. They united in the face of that potentially formidable opposition. Propelled by economic and class interests, the elites assaulted the remaining Indian and mestizo peasant lands in earnest.

Throughout most of the century, the Latin American patriarchs argued that the rural folk whose lives they controlled to a lesser or greater degree benefited from the distinct life-style of their estates. Interestingly enough, some recent revisionist scholarship posits a similar conclusion. Speaking of the peons on the Hacienda del Maguey, a livestock ranch of some 416 square miles in the state of Zacatecas, Mexico, Harry E. Cross concluded that they enjoyed a sufficient income and diet to maintain a satisfactory life-style. Evidence principally from the time around 1840 suggests that the Hacienda del Maguey was patriarchal and that the owners maintained a lively concern for the welfare of the workers. How widely one can expand this example to embrace larger areas of nineteenth-century Latin America awaits further research. For the moment, this example seems to call our attention to possible differences between the living standards of workers on some patriarchal estates and those of workers on the more commercial, export-oriented estates.

Further, at that period of time, the argument might be considered that the concentration of land and income in a few hands did not necessarily result in a diminishing quality of life for the majority so long as that majority still enjoyed some access to land and a satisfactory (or tolerable) relationship with the authorities and patriarchal class. Only when disproportionate energies and resources were invested to export a few items, when the export dominated the internal markets, when basic decisions favored the export sector as the dynamic center of the economy, was the quality of life of the majority threatened, largely because under those conditions they lost the use of land and were coerced into unfavorable labor relations with capitalist producers. The precedent external considerations took over internal ones inevitably strengthened dependency, which in turn diminished the quality of life of the majority.

The rapid importation of European ideas by the urban elites put the patriarchs on the defensive. In the early decades following independence they resisted successfully, stemming and at times reversing the tides of change. The clash of ideologies occasionally ignited physical combat between the liberals advocating some form of change and the conservatives who questioned the need. The United Provinces of Central America (1821–1839), into which the liberals had introduced some of the most advanced European ideas and practices, disintegrated under the impact of the liberal-conservative struggles. Similar struggles shook Brazil, 1831–1845, and nearly had the same centrifugal consequences. Shocked by the foreign ideas introduced by Liberal thinkers, part of the rural population in the Northeast rebelled in 1832. One of the rebel proclamations affirmed the backlanders' loyalty to class-conscious patriarchalism:

> The Liberals are against inequality, when from the time Christ assumed human form there has been inequality. . . . What the Liberals want is for the sons no longer to obey their fathers, nephews, their uncles, godchildren their godfather; what they want is, if she takes their fancy, to carry off another's daughter, or some pretty woman . . . proceeding in all against the law of Our Lord Jesus Christ. And, finally, they do not wish to obey the King, when God himself has said to the King that when his subjects fail to obey him he should destroy them with pestilence, hunger, and war.

Brazil escaped a fate similar to that of Central America partly by recourse to the patriarchal figure of the emperor. Vacated in 1831 by the abdication of Pedro I, the throne awaited the young Prince Pedro to reach the legal age of eighteen in 1844 before he could occupy it. The widening chaos of the Regency Period required other than formal constitutionalism to eradicate it. In response, the beleaguered parliament elevated the fourteen-year-old Pedro II to the throne, an unconstitutional act because he had not yet reached the age of majority. However, the coup calmed turbulent political waters. The presence of the young emperor on the throne provided the authority figure that reunified the sprawling empire. Hierarchy reigned; order returned. His early coronation reaffirmed the patriarchal principle, which had dominated Brazil for centuries. The escape from national disintegration slowed the impact of innovation at least for another generation.

Embattled defenders of older values, the patriarchs seldom emerged victorious during the remainder of the nineteenth century, although they proved to be tenacious compromisers. Any success they enjoyed tended to be more on the local rather than national levels. Still they did not desist even as the nineteenth merged into the twentieth century. One of the last national challenges of the patriarchs to the modernizers took place in Uruguay. In 1903–04 Aparicio Saravia led an uprising against José Batlle, in which the patriarchs tried to defend their Ibero-American values as the continent's first middle-class president guided Uruguay into the final stage of Europeanization. The patriarchs who followed Saravia barely knew the burgeoning port-capital of Montevideo, but they distrusted it as a haven of European immigrants who brought strange and undesirable ideas, styles, and customs into their land. To his followers, Saravia represented the Spanish tradition, the American heritage, Roman Catholicism, nationalist sentiments, fear of foreigners, and a trust in hierarchy, order, and respect for old values. On horseback, wearing a white poncho and sombrero, Saravia incarnated the gaucho legacy. The struggle between Batlle and Saravia symbolized the final conflict between those who favored a Europeanized future for Uruguay and those who sought to draw on a Uruguayan-American past as the model for the future. Batlle triumphed.

Saravia's quixotic challenge failed to deter those forces which, by the turn of the century, were in the process of reshaping much of Latin America: modernization, urbanization, and industrialization. Liberalism characterized politics, just as capitalism did economics. Both disturbed the patriarchs. In those regions where their lands were needed to produce exports, the patriarchs either converted to the new system or lost their lands to those attuned to the new realities. In the more remote or marginal areas, the patriarchs were spared that distress — at least for the time being.

The rural patriarchy did not fade from prominence without some literary laments, which furnish valuable insights into perceptions of change, alternatives to modernization, and fears of social disintegration believed — at least by some — to accompany change. Although wary of Europeanization, those literati mediated acceptance of change, a selective adoption of European values and techniques. They understood the attraction of Europe, yet appreciated the American experience as well. Somewhat naively perhaps, they sought to combine the best of both, and in that respect, they represented a third position between a Europeanized society on the one extreme and a folk society on the other.

The locale for the most romantic of the nineteenth-century novels, *María* (1867) by Jorge Isaacs, was a patriarchal estate in the Cauca Valley of Colombia. The novel has been translated into English under the name title. The author provided a wealth of detail, from which emerged his concept of the exemplary hacienda at midcentury. Orderly, hierarchical, harmonious, the well-run estate centered on the comfortable "big house" and patriarchal authority, which extended from the devoted slaves to the doting family. "Father" always knew best in that patrilineal setting. The novel's extreme popularity grew mainly from the ideal, but tragic romance it depicted, although some of its appeal must have come from the affinity it aroused in its readers for the idyllic country life where people and nature intertwined, where social roles were well defined and unquestionably accepted, where the values of human relationships took precedence over business and ambition, and where alienation apparently was unknown. Such patriarchal estates symbolized the model society to many Latin American writers, who frequently used them as backdrops for their stories.

In the last third of the century, Ignacio Manuel Altamirano in Mexico and Joaquín V. González in Argentina perceived their ideal society to be rural, well ordered, and patriarchal, and published books focusing directly on the patriarchal lifestyle. Altamirano idealized a mountain village in his *La Navidad en las Montañas* (*Christmas in the Mountains*, 1871). A simple, but good place, the village boasted of happiness, a high morality, harmony, and a patriarchal society, in which priest, mayor, school teacher, and village elders guided the local inhabitants. The author wove the patriarchal theme throughout the novel. He called the mayor "a patriarch of ancient times" and compared him on another occasion to "a Biblical patriarch." The old blind Indian, "Uncle Frank," he characterized as "a model strong man," who acted as the "natural counsellor" for the village. He elaborated:

The respect for his decisions reached such a point that a sentence which Uncle Frank pronounced in matters submitted to his patriarchal arbitration was considered unappealable. . . . The old Indian was the only one to whom, before the priest's coming, the people submitted their controversies about lands, the families carried their complaints, and asked for advice about marriage and matters of conscience. Never did a neighbor have to lament his decision, which was always based on a rigorous principle of justice. The priest, since his arrival, had found in Uncle Frank his most sufficient assistant in the improvements introduced into the village, as well as his most devoted and virtuous friend. For his part, the mountain patriarch professed for the priest extraordinary affection and admiration.

Thus Altamirano neatly sidestepped any problems of conflicting opinions, leadership rivalry, or jealousy between the village's traditional patriarch and the patriarch-figure of the more recently arrived priest. In fact, the harmony achieved between Indian and Spanish Mexico reinforced the patriarchal principle in Altamirano's village utopia. At the opening of the novel, the observer, himself an idealized military type, expressed his preference for patriarchy, commenting, "I had promised myself that I would end my journey in a small village of poor, but hospitable mountaineers who lived from the product of the soil and who enjoyed a relative well-being, thanks to their isolation from large, populous centers and to the goodness of their patriarchal customs." On the final page, he stated his satisfaction at having fulfilled his goal: "I myself forgot all my troubles and felt happy, contemplating that picture of simple virtue, and true, modest happiness, which in vain I had sought for in the midst of opulent cities and in a society agitated by terrible passions."

The patriarchal model did not eschew change. "Progress" had penetrated that mountain village. The priest introduced new crops, trees, and animals. A small grinding mill freed the women from the *metate*. The villagers built a school and hired a teacher, who in turn played an important and influential role in mediating further progress.

If priest and patriarch had helped to transform the isolated village into a model microcosm of soceity, so had the military. A long parable recounted the story of the errant Paul, who had turned bad, unworthy of the village and of the woman he wanted to marry. Military service reformed him, an apparent allusion to patriotic devotion to Mexico and its redeeming quality. Returning to his village, Paul became a model peasant: "In two years a great change had been effected in Paul's character and even in his physique. . . . He has made the most of some ideas about agriculture and horticulture and has put them into practice with such success that it is a pleasure to see his clearing, as he humbly calls it. It is not, in truth, a simple clearing, but a beautiful plantation with a bright future." It was the same rosy future to be shared by Paul—who won the hand of his beloved—and the village. An appropriately symbolic scene concluded the novel. Snow fell on Christmas day blanketing the village in a wrap of purity. The priest and military officer—obvious representatives of the two major institutions of nineteenth-century Mexico—looked on the village with satisfaction. They shared the joy. The past shaped the future. The village provided answers in the search for a satisfactory life, which the cities could not.

To Joaquín González, in *Mis Montañas* (1893), the rugged and quiet countryside with its noble people constituted the "real," the "original" Argentina. Interestingly enough, both González and Sarmiento were from La Rioja province, which both described in their books. If Sarmiento denigrated both the province and the gaucho, González idealized them. If Sarmiento hailed progress, González revered tradition: "Tradition is also a force; it is created by the sentiment and passion of the social mass and by a community of interests; it is an historic and philosophic element that explains great events; it is the history of peoples who have no history, the customs of peoples who have no formal laws." Drawing upon the Indian and African antecedents and contributions, tradition recognized more than an Iberian past and oriented the mestizo and mulatto toward their non-European heritage. In the rugged geography of La Rioja, tradition and patriarchy guaranteed a good life for the inhabitants. *Mis Montañas* like *La Navidad en la Montañas* offered a quiet counterpart to the hosannas acclaiming Europeanization. They can be read as nostalgic, but symbolic descriptions of an idealized rural society, quaint reminders of the past to the modernizers.

Less romantic authors used the rural past as a means to indict the present. Whatever faults the neofeudal latifundia might have had, the large estates seemed to some to have offered a better life than the burgeoning cities at the turn of the century. The behavior of the urban elites, new rich, and aspiring bourgeoisie particularly in a series of stock market booms and busts, which wrought financial havoc in Argentina, Brazil, and Chile during the final decade of the nineteenth century, disgusted part of the literati and prompted some serious questioning of the implications of modernization. In his *Casa Grande* (1908), Luis Orrego Luco cast a nostalgic — but not uncritical — glance at Chile's patriarchal past. The picture he drew of the estate of Leonidas Sandoval, father of one of the urbanized protagonists, contained no surprises: "The family since its arrival in Chile two centuries earlier had engaged in agriculture, possessing immense extensions of land on which the workers were considered like serfs of the Middle Ages and the owner gave orders with sovereign and unquestionable authority in a despotic fashion." For Orrego Luco, Sandoval represented a class, a patriarchal type that was disappearing. After a somewhat rudimentary education, Sandoval toured Europe with a priest as chaperon. Returning to Chile, he married a woman of his own social status and settled down to administering the family estate. Then, with some obvious glee, Orrego Luco revealed the connection between the landowning elite and politics:

It wasn't long before honors and political fortune came to him. He became a deputy in congress, where he constantly voted with the majority and accepted as articles of faith the opinions and caprices of the President of the Republic on whom depended both rain and sunshine. He spoke two or three times before the august assembly requesting protection for national industries or a higher tarriff on Argentine beef. For him, the very reason for politics was to serve his own personal interest whether it was to enact taxes that favored him, to push for the construction of a railroad, bridge, or road in his province, or to create a new job useful for some relative. What is more, for the members of the government Don Leonidas was the perfect friend. Although a man personally honorable, he voted without question the most shamelessly phony powers to the friends of the cabinet ministers and ardently defended the ministers in all their maneuvers. With such a social background and with a gentle appearance accented by a huge moustache, a serious yet relaxed air, a tranquil walk, discrete tone, and a certain reputation for being wealthy, he soon assumed a cabinet portfolio himself, which was a splendid accomplishment in those times when ministries lasted for years, not just months as they do now.

In a similar satirical vein, Orrego Luco presented his readers to other representatives of that eclipsed rural class, and none emerged from his pen more affable than Senador Peñalver, whose ancestral credentials were as impeccable as his visible means of support dubious. In one memorable statement the old gentleman confessed, "I have realized the political-economic ideal: I live in the best style possible with the least amount of effort. I live off the country." Those rural aristocrats might appear a bit picaresque, but alongside the wheeling and dealing of the corrupt, immoral urban elite they appeared harmless eccentrics whose way of life faded with the nineteenth century. The rural patriarchs who opposed or ignored modernization sooner or later became its victims.

Because the patriarchs regarded modernization with some suspicion and lived closely intertwined with rural folk societies and cultures, there often emerged some working relationship between the patriarchs and the folk. The benefits to the patriarchs were obvious: they had a ready labor force at their call. The folk extracted from the relationship the isolation and protection they sought to live in accordance with their established patterns.

CHAPTER SIX

The Folk Speak

If modernization threatened the traditional life-styles of the patriarchs, it entailed dire consequences for the rural masses who both opposed it and offered alternatives more suitable to their own needs. Few studies have considered those popular alternatives to the modernization pursued by the elites. Historians' customary fascination with the privileged as well as a lack of conventional documentation for the alternatives explain the silence. Because the overwhelming majority of the nineteenth-century Latin Americans were illiterate, they left few written accounts of their complaints, alternatives to Europeanization, or, for that matter, activities. That paucity of conventional documentation complicates but should not impede the search for popular preferences. However, it will require primarily the mastery of new sources and secondarily a reinterpretation of some of the more standard ones.

José Luis Romero ranks as one distinguished scholar who has attempted to come to grips with the popular alternatives to the politics of the dominant elite in nineteenth-century Argentina. While more sympathetic to the process of Europeanization in his study, *History of Argentine Political Thought,* he nonetheless devoted much more time than the usual token discussion to the countercurrent. He termed the popular alternative "inorganic democracy," which he defined thus:

> But for many reasons the provincials opposed the doctrinaire positions and the institutional principles of the enlightened group. To these ideas the people of the interior opposed a profoundly colonial mentality and local sentiments, by which they

demonstrated their new-born patriotism. . . . The people chose to obey the call of the caudillos of their class and of their own kind who sprang up on all sides, which gave support to a new authoritarianism that had some vaguely democratic characteristics since, in fact, the caudillo exalted the ideals of his people and carried to power with him a mandate to impose and defend their wishes. . . . The creoles were accustomed to the enjoyment of immense personal liberty. The desert assured them that freedom, although at the cost of their total exclusion from public life, which was run by the cities. When the revolutionary movement triumphed, the creoles wanted to transfer their feeling of indomitable liberty to political life, since mere obedience to laws appeared to them to be oppression. . . . From his unlimited sense of freedom was born a democratic desire to have their own chief rule.

The rustic rurals described by Romero had evolved a life-style that provided them with greater equality, security, and well-being within their own informal institutions than did the European pattern being imposed by Buenos Aires. While the society governed by those informal institutions might be classified by some as "more barbarous" than the Europeanized life of the cities, yet according to the conclusion of another renowned contemporary Argentine scholar, Roberto Cortés Conde, it was also "more democratic." Novelists, such as Leopoldo Lugones in his *La Guerra Gaucha* (1905), also have attempted to distill the essence of the meaning and function of those popular institutions, of which they intuitively approve. A 1942 Argentine film based on the novel and with the same title opened with a dedication to "Those Forgotten by History" and emphasized in the spirit of the novel that the harmony of the people with their geography forged the strength that defeated the Spaniards in the Argentine Andean region, 1814-1818, and guaranteed the independence of that interior region. The personification of those people was the caudillo Martín Güemes, revered by the humble mountain folk but held at arm's length by the official historians domiciled in the distant national capital. The mutual identification of people and caudillo exemplified the "inorganic democracy" that Romero found characteristic of the Argentine interior during much of the last century.

What Romero termed "inorganic democracy" can be related to "folk culture," a common way of life shared by the ordinary people, a general concept useful for the study of nineteenth-century Latin America. What distinguished the folk of nineteenth-century Latin America was their adherence to ideas and values formulated by the American experience over centuries. Because the folk drew cautiously and slowly from European sources, carefully mediating those outside influences, they did not embrace the values and ideology emanating from Europe—and later from North America—with the same enthusiasm and rapidity that generally characterized the welcome extended by the elites, wealthy, and aspiring middle class. The heavy infusion of modernization injected into national society by the urban elites in the nineteenth century, particularly during the last half—causing what was probably the greatest cultural confrontation in the New World since the early sixteenth century—shattered the relationship of the folk with their environment, a relationship already tenuous in some regions. That intrusion of broad change based on alien values constituted the major challenge of modernization to folk culture.

The folk stratum found in both the rural and urban communities composed the largest part of preindustrial Latin American society. Imbued with long traditions, those folk cultures had undergone a variety of changes and adaptations over the centuries. In fact, they were mediated cultures. To a greater or lesser degree, depending on the region, they drew from the Indian experience. For milennia, the Indians lived in hunting, fishing, gathering, agrarian, and village settings, modified in large regions of the Americas by the rise of kingdoms and empires and the attendant influence of the socioeconomic system of cities and villages. Still, the Indian monarchs shared similar customs, traditions, and values with their subjects; in blood they were one with the people. Even after the trauma of the Spanish and Portuguese conquests, there existed some degree of tolerance within Iberian institutions toward local customs, necessarily so in remote and marginal areas. Nonetheless, powerful Spanish and Portuguese influences reshaped the Indian societies since the dominated group was forced to adopt (or adapt) at least certain features of the dominant culture. Although transfers took place from the dominant to the subordinate cultures, the entire culture was not accepted by the Indians. They exercised considerable discretion. Once

José Rafael Carrera
(1814-1865)
(Source: Radio Times Hulton Picture
Library)

Juan Manuel de Rosas (1793-1877)
(Source: Organization of American States)

José Gaspar Rodríguez
de Francia
(1766-1840)

(Source: Vivian Trías, *El Paraguay de Francia el Supremo a la Guerra de la Triple Alianza.* Buenos Aires: Crisis, 1975)

Francisco Solano López
(1826-1870).
Reputedly the last
photograph taken of the
Paraguayan caudillo.

(Source: Maria Concepción L. de Chaves, *Madame Lynch.* Buenos Aires: Peuser, 1957)

Teresa Urrea (1873-1903),
The Saint of Cabora
(Source: William Curry Holder, *Teresita.*
Owings Mills, Md.: Stemmer House, 1978)

Female Guerrilla, Panama, c. 1901.
The caption under this photograph
read, "One of the Amazons who
reached high rank in an insurgent
army."
(Source: Hezekiah Butterworth, *A Popular
History of South America.* New York:
Doubleday, 1904)

An Argentine Gaucho, c. 1868.
(Source: The Havey Collection, Library of
Congress)

The peach seller. An Argentine lithograph, 1830, by César H. Bacle.

The country girl. An Argentine lithograph, 1840, by Adolfo d'Hastrel.

A drawing of Canudos, Brazil, c. 1896.

Dancing the popular
zamacueca, Lima, 1856. The
drawing is by Bonaffé.

A Brazillian slave hut, c. 1830.
(Source: Jean Ferdinand Denis, *Brasilien*. Stuttgart: Schweizerbart, 1836-1838)

Interior of a Brazilian slave hut, c. 1822.
(Source: Jean-Baptiste Debret, *Voyage Pittoresque et Historique au Brésil*. Paris: Didot, 1834-1839)

A family in front of their hut, Puerto Cabello, Venezuela, c. 1880.
(Source: Curtis Collection, Library of Congress)

A European peasant immigrant family in Uruguay, c. 1900.
(Source: Organization of American States)

Indian laborers on an Argentine estate in Tucumán, c. 1918.
(Source: Organization of American States)

Patagonian chiefs, Argentina, c. 1910.
(Source: Organization of American States)

the initial impact of the dominant groups on the subordinated groups had been felt and the latter had accepted from the former the cultural innovations, the Indians became less receptive to change. Perhaps the dominant European cultures were more pronounced on the Africans, who had been removed from their cultural environments and dispersed widely throughout the Americas. European peasant folk cultures, too, were transferred to the New World, where they interacted with the Afro-Indian folk cultures. As the new Latin American nations took political shape in the first half of the nineteenth century, the governments, largely European in spirit, confronted viable folk cultures, which had amalgamated Indian, African, and European traditions. From the vantage point of the Europeanized elites of the capital cities, those folk cultures and specifically the folk societies, organized groups of individuals characterized by a folk culture, stood as barriers to the creation of the desired "modern" state, an argument well summarized by Sarmiento.

Folk culture was based on a common language, heritage, beliefs, and means of facing daily life. It instilled a feeling of unity, loyalty, and tradition within the folk, more intuitive than codified, although folk wisdom, folk poetry, and folk tales gave verbal insight into them.

In the nineteenth century, particularly during the first half, the folk culture thrived within folk societies in the countryside and in the rural villages. Those folk societies comprised small, isolated communities, which manifested a strong sense of group solidarity. The common folk culture bound people together into an intradependent, intimate, and largely self-sufficient society. A well-defined moral order in which each person knew his role and the interrelationships of individuals characterized the folk society. The folk held more to fixed laws of behavior and human existence, a contrast with the teleological bent of the Western mind. A unity of feeling and action accompanied a sense of harmony with the environment to satisfy inner needs. The combination of unity, harmony, and satisfaction comprised the soul of the people.

Education within those societies emphasized the individual's relationship to the group and inculcated in children a moral behavior honored by the community. In short, the result was to recreate in the child the patterns of the adult.

Education provided continuity by passing on and maintaining tradition.

The incentives to work and to trade originated in tradition, moral dictates, community obligations, and kinship relations. In those essentially nonmaterialistic cultures, economic decisions took second place to social considerations. The system worked sufficiently well to provide the folk with employment, food, housing, community spirit, and reasonable satisfaction. Life-styles were simple; hardships were common; the disadvantages were obvious, at least to the outsider. Such life-styles repulsed the Europeanized elites of the cities. Indeed, the behavior of the folk could be neither understood nor explained within the framework of Western thought. It did not evolve exclusively from the Iberian experience, nor did it acknowledge the influence of the liberal ideology of the Enlightenment or the French Revolution. Within their own experience, however, the societies seem to have provided adequately for their members. Modest as their standards of living might have been, they deteriorated under the accelerating modernization, which first modified and then partially eradicated the folk societies of the nineteenth century.

An interplay between folk cultures and the Europeanizing cities always existed. Within the cities themselves folk cultures, although not folk societies, thrived, characterized by a symbiotic Europeanization. Esteban Echeverría drew an unflattering portrait of the folk element of Buenos Aires in his novelette *La Matadora* ("The Slaughterhouse", written about 1838 but not published until 1871). Not surprisingly that vocal member of the Generation of 1837 decried the urban folk as a threat to Europeanization. They were the "urban barbarians." Under pressures from the Europeanized elites who succeeded in effecting economic growth, urbanization, industrialization, and modernization in some parts of Latin America, the folk societies diminished, although the folk cultures, as in the past, accommodated to much of the change and continued to exist in forms distinct from those earlier in the century.

Some of the leaders selected by the folk played significant roles in regional and national life. Nineteenth-century history, particularly the half-century following independence, offers a number of fascinating examples of such popular leaders, often referred to as caudillos—although, of course, not all caudillos were folk leaders. As far as we can tell, the folk expected their leader to represent and strengthen their unity, express their soul, personify their values, and increase their harmony; in short, to be as one with the people he led. Their caudillo recognized and understood the distinctive way of life of the folk and acted in harmony with it. In the eyes of the people, he inculcated the local, regional or national values—traditional values —with which most of the people felt comfortable. He exuded a natural, a charismatic, leadership of the majority, who found in him an adviser, a guide, a leader, a protector, a patriarch in whom they entrusted their interests. They surrendered power to him; he exercised it for their benefit. He embodied collective will; he encarnated authority. The fusion of leader and people had to be nearly perfect (that is, perceived by those involved as nearly perfect), and when the interplay existed both people and leader sensed, valued, and honored their interdependency. In his discussion of leadership and folk society, José Carlos Mariátegui ascribed to the leader the roles of "interpreter and trustee." Mariátegui concluded, "His policy is no longer determined by his personal judgment but by a group of collective interests and requirements." The leader seemingly arose from and blended with his physical and human environment. Thus identified with America, he contrasted sharply with the Europeanized leaders imposed by the elites.

The popularity of such caudillos is undeniable. Their governments rested on a base of folk culture, drew support and inspiration from the folk, and expressed, however vaguely, their style. Under the leadership of such caudillos, the masses apparently felt far more identification with government than they ever did under the imported political solutions advocated by the intellectuals and the elite. On many occasions the folk displayed support of their caudillos by fighting tenaciously to protect them from the Europeanized elites and/or foreign invaders.

Juan Batista Alberdi, probably more than anyone else in the nineteenth century, studied the psychology of the relationship of popular caudillos with the masses, and he concluded that the people regarded a popular caudillo as "guardian of their traditions," the defender of their way of life. He insisted that such leaders constituted "the will of the popular masses . . . the immediate organ and arm of the people . . . the caudillos are democracy." He reiterated frequently in his writing the equation of the popular caudillo with democracy:

> Thus, the system of caudillos appears in America in the form of democracy and together they develop and progress. Artigas, López, Güemes, Quiroga, Rosas, Peñaloza, as chiefs, heads, and authorities are the product of their people, their most spontaneous and genuine personification. Without any other authorization than that, without finances, without resources, they have guided the people with more power than the governments possess.

If the folk obeyed unreservedly those popular leaders, the caudillos in turn born the obligation to protect and to provide for the welfare of the people. The ruled and ruler were responsible to and for each other, a personal relationship challenged in the nineteenth century by the more impersonal capitalist concept that a growing gross national product would provide best for all.

Imbued with European political ideas, inheritors of the Enlightenment, the elites scoffed at the concepts represented by the folk caudillos; "barbarians" was the epithet they hurled. Their own political concepts, always highly theoretical, focused on the separation and balance of powers, equality, federalism, and other political ideas that seemed in vogue in the United States and/or Europe. Yet, their practice embraced a mixture of both their own *caudillismo* and liberal democracy, with inclinations more toward the former. They, too, felt most comfortable, certainly more secure, with a caudillo, albeit one who represented their new values and protected their old institutions. Simón Bolívar, who authored more than one constitution, recognized the vitality of and need for just such an omniscient, omnipotent, and omnipresent leader. Speaking of his 1826 constitution for Bolivia, he revealed, "The President of the Republic shall come to be in our constitution like the sun, fixed in the center, giving life to the universe." But Bolívar's universe contrasted with that of the folk and therein lay the potential for cultural conflict.

In his biography of Aparicio Saravia, Manuel Gálvez noted that his death in 1904 during his struggle against President José Batlle of Uruguay, the city, and foreign influence, marked the end of the era of the caudillo on horseback in the Americas. Gálvez tried to distill what Saravia represented and concluded he personified gaucho liberty, Iberian and Roman Catholic tradition, nationalist sentiments, distrust of foreign influence, an order based on hierarchy, and respect for moral values. In short, he incarnated what was Spanish and profoundly American in the Uruguayan people. Saravia well represented the not unusual alliance of folk and patriarchs who shared traditional rural values and were cautious of urban and foreign ways. Such alliances obviously crossed class lines, reemphasizing again the cultural nature of this nineteenth-century conflict. The hazy class lines complicate the application of customary political labels to those alliances, since the folk favored community arrangements that might suggest a rustic socialism, while the patriarchs represented, depending on one's viewpoint and/or emphasis, a type of neofeudalism or patrimonialism or neocapitalism.

Argentine history offers excellent examples of popular and populist caudillos: Juan Facundo Quiroga, Martín Güemes, Felipe Varela, and Angel Vicente Peñaloza, to mention only a few obvious ones. Certainly the caudillo of greatest import was Juan Manuel de Rosas, who, in one way or another, dominated Argentina from 1829 until 1852. The masses demonstrated their loyalty by their willingness to fight for him for nearly a quarter of a century. Rosas suffered defeat and exile only when the elites enlisted the Brazilian army to unite with them to overthrow him. The concepts of these caudillos as the popular leaders of the masses and of the mutual devotion of leader and masses were as difficult for most of the Europeanized elite to accept as were the popular leaders. The identification of the masses with Rosas explains in part the negative role assigned that caudillo in official Argentine historiography as well as the historical obscurity to which a dozen local leaders have been banished.

Three other examples of the popular caudillo exercising national power were José Gaspar Rodríguez de Francia of Paraguay (1814–1840), Rafael Carrera of Guatemala (1839–1865), and Manuel Belzu of Bolivia (1848–1855). The ordinary people supported those caudillos, identifying with them and feeling they benefited from them.

The sources for the study of an alternative history, that of the folk rather than the well-documented history of the elites, have survived to some degree in folklore. Argentine folklore, for example, including gaucho poetry, offers evidence of popular support for "inorganic democracy," with the local caudillos regarded as the defenders of the people's rights and preferences. While praising the rustic virtues of the countryside, the folklore denigrated the cities filled with foreigners and subject to European influences. True, critics detect a defense of the neofeudalism, which to them characterized parts of the countryside, but another aspect of the rural area was the opportunity for the gaucho to acquire his own string of ponies and herd of cattle, thus a social mobility and flexibility contrary to feudalism as well as unusual later under Argentine capitalism. Also, the great space and isolation of the pampas engendered freedom and individuality among the gauchos. Certainly until midcentury an informality of relationships existed in the pampas, which the integration of Argentine beef and wheat into the world market later destroyed. Much of the pertinent folklore reminisces nostalgically about that informality.

Brazilian folk narrative, derived from Ibero-Afro-Amerindian sources, identified the rich as "bad" and the society dominated by the wealthy as a "world apart" in which the poor could not hope to occupy anything but a subservient position. The Mexican *corridos* also comment on social distinctions, attacking the morals, habits and dress of the elite. Significantly those corridos emphasized violence and thereby contributed to the conclusion that violence was one of the most notable characteristics of nineteenth-century Latin America. As an intricate part of Mexican life, "of, by and for the *pueblo*," the corridos offer a magnificent insight into the popular mind as well as important historical documents for the study of the masses. The otherwise elusive public opinion they preserve proves to be radically different from the better-known ideology of the elite. Apparently the folk poets were worthy representatives of the people. Their poems provided a matrix of homogeneity and common identification for the masses over a broad geographic area, thereby imparting a solidarity comparable to the well-forged unity of the elites with their standardized ideology, of which the historiography of the nineteenth century discussed in chapter three serves as the perfect example.

Nathan Wachtel has supplied an ingenious methodology for the study of Indian dances in his book *The Vision of the Vanquished,* which explains how they express part of the collective psychology of the Indians. Tracing the history of the various dances of the conquest through the centuries, Wachtel affirmed that they bear the impress of the trauma of that event. Periodic and ritual repetition of the dances satisfy the participants since the dances reinforce their interpretation of the past and give vent to feelings of repressed hostility.

The large Indian population of Latin America tenaciously resisted Westernization. The Indians constituted a majority in fully a third of the nations during the past century and a sizeable minority in many of the others. They showed every evidence of preferring their own customs to those of the distant metropolis or the isolated capital city and their communal life to the new nation-state. A pervasive passive resistance transcended generations. Many Indians refused to dress like Europeans. While acknowledging Roman Catholicism, they often retained parts of their own religion, establishing a syncretism, which in some cases infiltrated the European community. They participated in the local, not national, economy. They revered their own values and ignored those radiating from Europe. In fact, they often juxtaposed to the official values their own wisdom. From the capital city may have reverberated through the constitution and laws such echoes of the Enlightenment as "All men are created equal," but local wisdom noted in proverbs, "For the rich who robs the garden there is no law, no judge, no prison; but if a poor man steals a crumb the thief goes to jail."

Passive resistance to Westernization often gave way to rebellion as the Indians demonstrated their willingness to defend their way of life from further inroads of Europeanization. Rebellion was common in the nineteenth century. It signified a defiance, resistance, or reaction to a particular set of circumstances, and its objective was to restructure those circumstances so that they would favor the rebels. It most often took the form of peasant tumult against local landlords or local governmental officials for specific reasons and brought about by specific causes. In other words, it was not aimed against the nation and/or its institutions as such. The question why revolution—a total change of the institutional structures that would have to be either on a national level or through secession of a region— was rare or nonexistent remains open to discussion, but its near absence (a case might be made for revolution in Mexico, 1810–1815; Guatemala, 1838–1865; Paraguay, 1814–1870; Yucatan in the last half of the century; and perhaps others) must relate to the limited or local view of the folk. Since official historiography has been reticent to recognize popular wrath and to discuss the implications of it, little attention has been given to Indian resistance and alternatives. Guatemala provides a handy and useful example of Indian resistance and temporary success as well as the subsequent silence accorded it in the history texts.

At midcentury the population of Guatemala numbered less than a million. The overwhelming majority was Indian, nominally Roman Catholic, non-Spanish speaking, and minimally influenced by three centuries of Spanish rule. The Spaniards had respected much of the indigenous cultures. However, independence in 1821 elevated to power a segment of the elite that had imbibed the heady wines of Enlightenment thought and, judging the Indians to be backward, terminated the benign neglect of the crown. According to the simile of the times, Indianism marked the appropriate infancy of Guatemala that would mature to adulthood nurtured on a European diet. In short, if Guatemala were to progress, then the Indians had to be Europeanized.

During the decade of the 1830s, the government of Mariano Gálvez energetically set out to remodel Guatemala in an effort to eradicate Indian institutions in favor of the latest European ones. As elsewhere in the hemisphere, the government favored European immigration as the guarantee for progress. In a moment of generosity—or desperation—in 1834, the government awarded nearly all the public lands to foreign companies that promised to people Guatemala with Europeans. The area conceded covered nearly three-quarters of Guatemala. Regarding the Indian communal lands as an unprogressive remnant of the past, the government proceeded to put them up for sale, a bargain eagerly acquired by a growing and ambitious mestizo class as well as by foreigners. New laws forced the Indians to build roads and ports and reestablished the burdensome head tax on them in order to finance the infrastructure that would integrate Guatemala more completely with Europe. At every turn the Indians faced increasingly heavy taxes and workloads, confiscation of their lands, and deprecation of their cultural values. At the same time the government intensified its attacks on the Roman Catholic clergy as retrograde and legislated to reduce its influence. To the Indian communities, on the other hand, the clergy remained as their last protector from a hostile, Europeanized government. They perceived any decrease in the Church's powers as an increase in their own vulnerability to exploitation or destruction. Clearly, by debilitating the only defender of the Indian masses, the elites enhanced their own position. The elites understood the organizational strength of the Roman Catholic Church to surpass that of the nascent political institutions they fostered and welcomed the opportunity to weaken a rival. Furthermore, the property confiscated from the Church ended up in the hands of the secular elites, increasing their wealth, prestige, and ultimately power. The many grievances of the Indians reached a climax in 1837 with the outbreak of a virulent cholera epidemic, the final proof to the Indians that the government sought to eliminate them in order to give their lands to immigrants. At that point a popular revolt, one of the major ones in nineteenth-century Latin America, broke out, and Rafael Carrera, a mestizo with firm roots in the Indian community, took the leadership.

Among the many things that popular rebellion signified, it voiced the refusal of the Indians to countenance any further exploitation and destruction through Europeanization. Their alternative was to be left alone by the elites of Guatemala City so that they could live unmolested according to the dicta of their own culture. They rejected education, culture, economy, and laws that would Europeanize them to the extent of integrating them into a capitalist economy centered in Europe. They chose to withdraw, to isolate themselves; and withdrawal was, and remains, a common reaction of the Indians before the Europeans. But withdrawal signified rebellion in regions where the elites depended on those Indians for labor and taxes. Carrera understood the Indian position; he sympathized with the desires of the Indians; and he rose to power on their strength.

During the generation 1838–1865, in which Rafael Carrera

dominated Guatemala, he respected the native cultures, protected the Indians insofar as that was possible, and sought to incorporate them into his government. His modest successes in these efforts assume greater significance when compared to the disastrous conditions suffered by the Indian majority during the decades of liberal, Europeanized governments that preceded and followed the Carrera period. That popular caudillo, totally unschooled in foreign theories, was a practical man who knew Guatemala and its peoples well. He had traveled and lived in many parts of the nation, always among the humble folk whom he understood. He drew from his Guatemalan experiences, a marked contrast to the elites seduced by European experiences and theories. Carrera appreciated the Indians' opposition to the process of Europeanization imposed by the Liberals. He regarded it as his principal duty to allow "the people to return to their customs, their habits, and their particular manner of living." The government, he affirmed, had the obligation of representing the majority of the people and of offering "a living example of virtue, equity, prudence, and justice." Those principles seem to have guided much of his long administration.

While Carrera repudiated the radical ideas of the Liberals, he never eschewed change. He believed it must come slowly and within the social context, a change acceptable to the people and not forced on them. An editorial in *El Noticioso* as late as 1861 decried the wholesale importation of innovations from Europe and the United States and went on to advocate the evolution from a colonial past to a national present through careful deliberation. Such gradualism generally characterized the Guatemalan government under Carrera. Revisionist studies now credit that government with respecting Indian customs and protecting the rural Indians. The president held that the art of governing well sprang from the "formation of a government of the people and for the people." Accordingly, the government officially abandoned the Liberals' goal to incorporate the Indians into Western civilization. One even could argue that under Carrera the government was "Indianized." Indians and particularly mestizos, all of relatively humble classes, participated directly in the government, holding such exalted offices, in addition to the presidency of course, as the vice-presidency, ministries, governorships and high military ranks. The army became nearly an Indian institution. The Carrera government was unique in Latin America for providing the political ascendancy of the once-conquered race. Significantly the "white" political monopoly was broken and never again could the minute white aristocracy govern Guatemala alone. Fundamental to Carrera's government was the decree of August 16, 1839, to protect the Indians. Commenting on the new decree, *El Tiempo* editorialized, "It is the object of public interest not only to protect the most numerous class in our society but also to encourage it to improve its customs and civilization, which can be done by providing it with the means to acquire and increase its small property holdings and industry by which it lives." Such were the intentions of the Carrera government.

The government generally succeeded in carrying out those intentions. Governmental decrees were translated into Indian languages and "protectors" appointed to serve the Indian communities. Carrera himself regularly received Indian delegations and seems to have traveled frequently in order to visit with the Indians. To lift some of the economic burden from the impoverished majority, he reduced taxes on foodstuffs and abolished the head tax. Further, he excused the Indians from contributing to the loans the government levied from time to time to meet fiscal emergencies. On the other hand, the government did not hesitate to reinstate the former alcoholic beverage controls, which included higher taxation, one means Carrera had of both increasing revenues and imposing a greater morality on the countryside. By removing many of the taxes on the Indians, which were paid in the official currency circulating in Europeanized Guatemala, the government lessened the need for the indigenous population to enter the monetary economy, thus reducing the pressure on them to work on the estates. The Indians, then, could devote that time and energy to their own agricultural and community needs.

The government took a pragmatic view of education. It encouraged a basic education, believing that for the majority of the inhabitants a simple education emphasizing reading, writing, and Christian doctrine would suffice. Higher education was available, primarily in the capital, for those desiring it. In the almost exclusively Indian Department of Sacatepequez, a decree of 1849 required each village to establish a school for boys to learn reading, writing, arithmetic, religion, and moral principles. "As soon as funds are available, those municipalities will establish schools for girls." Scholarships were to be available to defray expenses of poor children.

Of all the efforts made in behalf of the Indians none surpassed the protection of Indian lands, the return of land to Indian communities, and the settlement of land disputes in their favor. The government declared in 1845 that all who worked unclaimed lands should receive them. What was even more unusual it enforced the decree. It was decided in 1848 and repeated the following year that all pueblos without *ejidos* were to be granted them without cost, and if population exceeded available lands, then lands elsewhere were to be made available to any persons who voluntarily decided to move to take advantage of them. In 1851, Carrera decreed that "the Indians are not to be dispossessed of their communal lands on any pretext of selling them," a decree strengthened a few months later by prohibiting the divestment of any pueblos of their ejidos for any reason. Carrera thus spoke forcefully and effectively to the most pressing problem of Latin America: the overconcentration of land in the hands of the elite and the need for the rural masses to have land to cultivate. The Carrera decades witnessed increasing agrarian diversification, an escape from the monoculture that had characterized agriculture for so long. The intent was not so much to increase exports as to insure a plentiful supply of food in the marketplace at prices the people could afford. From the evidence at hand it would seem that the quality of life for the Indian majority improved during the Carrera years.

While some studies have concentrated recently on the government and programs of Carrera, scant attention has been given to the philosophical views of Carrera and of his government concerning the Indians and the many complex problems of a dual society. As has been stated, the government realized its strength rested upon Indian support and certainly exerted efforts to protect and help the Indians, but the impression often remains that Carrera acted more from realpolitik than conviction, that he was more paternalistic than egalitarian.

Those paternal and pragmatic aspects of governmental policy seem most readily evident, and it should not be surprising since Guatemalans inherited centuries of institutionalized Spanish paternalism. Furthermore, the anthropological thought emanating from Europe in the nineteenth century ranked the Indian as inferior, and accordingly even the most benevolent Latin American governments exercised paternalism over the native inhabitants but withheld any recongition of real equality. Indeed, the policies of most governments confronting the Indian populations were to insist on their absorption into the Westernizing patterns or their eradication. The Carrera government offered a refreshing contrast. Despite the intellectual climate in which Carrera governed, there exists some justification for speculating that certain policy makers, among them the president, maintained an unusually open and enlightened attitude toward the Indians, rare anywhere in the nineteenth century and a harbinger of ideas that would take another century to germinate. The evidence is still spotty and begs further research. These suggestions are based on some scattered—but neglected—evidence. First and foremost are the actions of the government, which, unlike so many later governments in Latin America, acted for the benefit of the Indians and to a large extent in conformity with Indian demands. But there were also some philosophical pronouncements scattered throughout the Carrera years which provided a glimpse of official thinking.

Carrera's *Informe* to the legislature in 1848 remains one of his major policy statements. In it he criticized the elites' abuses of the Indians, displayed a laudable understanding of Indian psychology, and expressed his concern for and sympathy with the Indian peoples, who, he emphasized, composed "two-thirds of the Republic's population." In his view, "humanity" and "common sense" required a fair treatment of that majority, which would be best served by the old laws and practices with which they were accustomed. Similar views were discussed on other occasions to reveal on the one hand that official philosophy did not change through the years, but that on the other hand it was difficult to overcome prejudices apparently ingrained in the Europeanized segment of the population. *El Noticioso* carried a significant essay entitled "El Antagonismo de Razas" in 1862, which expressed the official attitude in the

later years of the Carrera period. While succumbing to the conclusion that European civilization was "superior" and thus
subscribing to the racial implications of that conclusion, the
essay warned that to accept the Anglo-Saxon version of European civilization would condemn the Indians to extermination,
a condition unacceptable to the writer. The solution seemed
to be the introduction of European civilization as it filtered
through the more acceptable Spanish experience and within
the framework of Spanish Europe and Indian America, Guatemala could forge its own civilization.

Within a month, *El Noticioso* returned to that theme in a
clever essay, "Fantasia," signed by Miguel Boada y Balmes.
The author called for nothing less than equal rights for the
Indians, a singular voice in a hemisphere that at that time
adamantly denied everything to the original inhabitants: "the
ideal of the present is the moral, and to a certain point physical, emancipation of the Indian, his freedom to enjoy the right
universally admitted to be human. . . ." The author based his
arguments on the philosophical views favoring the equality of
all men, on Christianity, on social justice, and on the brute
economic reality that the Indians produced the wealth others
enjoyed.

A further testimony to Carrera's concern for the Indians'
well-being and to the interdependency of the Indian communities and the president came from the United States minister to
Guatemala (1861–64), Elisha Oscar Crosby. An enthusiastic
admirer of Carrera, the minister observed:

> He was always mindful of the rights of the common people,
> especially of the Indians. They would come sometimes in dele-
> gations of hundreds from distant provinces to lay their griev-
> ances before him, and he would sit patiently and hear all their
> complaints and have them inquired into, and direct redress
> and remedies. He had the most perfect control and confidence
> of all that aboriginal population. I suppose in forty-eight hours
> he could have assembled a hundred thousand of those Indians
> to his assistance if he had needed them. . . .

The characteristics marking the Carrera experience as unique
in Indo-America are the respect the government extended to
Indian cultures and the reluctance to push the Indian population into Europeanizing.

A willingness to respect Indian customs did not eliminate the government's attention to progress. In the relative calm of the last decade and a half of the Carrera government, the dual society both preserved the past and flirted with the future. During the closing years of the period, the newspapers commented frequently on the satisfactory pace of "progress" and "advancement ," not hesitating to applaud the maturing "civilization" of Guatemala. President Carrera himself once had reminded the legislature that when he entered office his enemies expected "barbarism" to envelop the country but that he consistently had fostered "culture and civilization."

In the last decade of the century, the novelist Manuel Cabral, writing under the pseudonym of Felipe de Jesus, provided a unique insight into Guatemala City during the final Carrera years. The author repeatedly reminisced in his novel *María, Historia de una Mártir* (1897) that those were happy years for the republic. He made the comparison between his and those times in the following terms:

> The beautiful capital of the Republic was around 1860. . . . one of the most tranquil and consequently placidly enchanting cities of Spanish America. Foreigners had not yet taken possession of it and therefore had not introduced those European customs that — let me say it frankly — if they have brought us some advantages have caused us on the other hand much trouble. . . . No, let's not completely foresake the past. Perhaps we find many improvements in our present style of living but at the same time we miss many things that we have lost and whose loss now grieves us. We accept, as we will always accept, with pleasure everything that represents a positive advancement, but at the same time we energetically reject everything that tends to diminish the happiness of the people. Peace of mind, tranquility in the home, purity of customs, public morality are advantages a thousand times more precious than all the inventions and discoveries of modern science. . . . A frenzy for business and with it questionable speculations had not yet invaded us in those bygone days; there was no luxury but there was decency; commerce was limited but more honorable . . . and consequently if misery did exist it was on a very small scale. National industries flourished and prospered even if at a modest rhythm. Today all that has disappeared almost completely because of the importation of European goods. What we once produced ourselves we now import. True, it

> might be more attractive but it doesn't last as long and is
> therefore more costly. . . . From such exploitation, from such
> abuse of our hospitality, our poverty has arisen. What does it
> matter if today there is greater happiness in certain circles if
> on the other hand the tears flow abundantly in the suburbs of
> our beautiful capital? . . . In those days the number of poor
> families was few; today they are the majority.

The novel is significant as a nostalgic glance at the Carrera
years, judging them representative of a benign period in Guatemalan history when the majority probably lived better than
at any other period in the century.

In the fascinating if overly romanticized plot, María, at one
time a member of a small, rising middle class, identified with
the Indians. The novel and its chief protagonist praise the older
values, those associated with the Spanish but more particularly
with the Indian past. Criticism fell on the elites depicted as
wicked, alienated from traditional values, and corrupted by
European influences. María confided to her family's former
maid, an Indian, "I know that you and alongside of you all the
humble daughters of the people, to whose class I belong with
all my heart from this day forward, are more generous, better,
more unselfish, and nobler than many of those proud aristocrats who believe themselves degraded if they deign to speak a
word to us." On that level, the novel symbolizes the relationship
of the races in Guatemala, the white dominating and exploiting
the Indian, although in the concluding pages María was vindi-
cated and the wicked aristocracy was punished. The interpretive possibilities are far-reaching. Given the time and the place,
Cabral made a strong and unusual statement on class con-
sciousness and conflict. Indeed, the author's dedicatory words
alert the reader to these sympathies: "To the Working Class.
To the virtuous working women who selflessly struggle against
the injustices of destiny and suffer with heroic resignation the
humiliations to which their condition subjects them." That
dedication suggests an interpretation of the novel on two time
levels: the vindication of María and thus the Indians during
the Carrera period in which the novel was set and a denunciation of the exploitation and degradation of the Indian thereafter when the novel and its dedication were written.

The Indian victory under Carrera proved to be as transitory as the gauchos' under Rosas. The death of Carrera in 1865 reinvigorated the elites' effort to wield power, and they succeeded under the leadership of another and different type of caudillo, Justo Rufino Barrios, 1873-1885. Positivist in orientation, President Barrios duly emphasized order and material progress. Under the Liberal reforms of the post-1871 period, capitalism made its definitive entry into Guatemala, which meant large-scale exportation of coffee with all the attendant consequences for that agrarian economy. The government rushed to import foreign technicians, ideas, and manufactured goods. It did not hesitate to contract foreign loans to pay for the Europeanization. The improvement of roads from the highland plantations to the ports and then the construction of the much desired railroads first to the Pacific and later to the Atlantic accelerated coffee production and integrated Guatemala into the world market system more closely than ever. As elsewhere the new railroads were owned and operated by foreigners and paid handsome profits to overseas investors. The burden of financing the railroads as well as the other accoutrements of progress inevitably fell on the local poor.

Spiraling coffee production for export had several long-range, negative consequences. For one thing, it diminished the amount of land, labor, and capital available to produce food for local consumption. Wheat harvests especially declined. Monoculture again became a dominant characteristic of the economy. To create the necessary work force on the coffee fincas, the Indians were forced, under a burdensome system of *mandamientos,* to become wage laborers. Meanwhile the government did not hesitate to concede to private landowners many lands on which the Indians had lived and worked for generations. By a variety of means the large estates encroached on the Indians' communal lands. As a consequence the economic and social position of the Indian majority declined. Anthropologists have recorded the negative effect of the coffee plantations on the indigenous cultures, which have never recovered from the shock. The pitiful conditions of the Indians prompted Francisco Lainfiesta, a minister in the Barrios government, to mount an eloquent defense of them in his novel *A*

Vista de Pájaro (1879). Later, in his novel *Edmundo* (1896), José A. Beteta lamented the degradation of the "miserable Indians bent beneath the weight of their rude work . . . who seemed to cry over the loss of the adored land that belonged to their grandfathers and to sigh for the liberty robbed from them."

The judgments of the Barrios period and the Liberal reforms inevitably point to the material changes, the prosperity of the elites, and the transformation of Guatemala City into a pseudo-European capital. To balance those accomplishments were a return to monoculture, declining food production for local consumption, rising foreign debt, forced labor, debt peonage, the growth of the latifundia, and the greater impoverishment of the majority. Reflecting once again the common historiographical bias, library shelves display ample biographical studies of the two nineteenth-century "modernizers," Gálvez and Barrios, while historians continue to ignore Rafael Carrera.

During the period Carrera governed Guatemala, Bolivia, another predominately Indian country, witnessed the singular leadership of Manuel Belzu. He remains a highly controversial figure about whom too little still is known. Erratic assessments of him damn or laud his government. The official historiography tends to be negative. On the other hand, at least one foreign observer, M. León Favre-Clavairon, a French consular official who visited Bolivia several times during the Belzu administration, gave the president high marks but observed that he had great difficulty in putting his ideas into action because of the fierce opposition of his enemies.

Belzu played a complex political role combining the forces of populism, nationalism, and revolution in ways they would not be used again in Latin America for over half a century. He built an effective power base of campesino and urban artisan support, which brought him to the presidency in 1848 and sustained him until he peacefully left the presidential palace in 1855. Dispossessed and impoverished as their counterparts were throughout Latin America, the artisans and campesinos rallied to Belzu probably because his novel rhetoric spoke directly to their needs and certainly because of a series of wildly popular actions he took. Their leader encouraged the organization of the first modest labor unions, ended some free-trade practices, terminated some odious monopolies, abolished slavery, and valorized the Indian past, permitting the landless Indians to take over the lands they worked for the latifundista elite. Often vague, frequently unsuccessful, his varied programs nonetheless won popular support. To his credit, President Belzu seemed to have understood the basic problems bedeviling Bolivia: foreign penetration and manipulation of the economy and the alienation of the Indians' land.

Under the intriguing title "To Civilize Oneself in Order To Die of Hunger," a series of articles in the weekly newspaper *El Estandarte,* founded in La Paz in 1852 and subsidized by Belzu, highlighted a vigorous campaign denouncing free trade and favoring protectionism. The paper argued that free trade deprived Bolivian workers of jobs while enriching foreigners and importers. It advocated "protectionism" as a means to promote local industry and thereby to benefit the working class, goals that had the obvious support of the president. Intellectuals like José Maria Dalence clamored for protection of local products, pointing out that Bolivia was in no position to heed the European theorists of free trade. Such ideas suited well-industrialized nations, he argued, but inevitably handicapped backward states like Bolivia. At one point, Belzu apparently tried to nationalize import commerce, but lack of credit and capital thwarted his efforts.

Free trade bore some responsibility for the nation's poor agricultural performance. A chronic imbalance of trade between 1825 and 1846 had cost Bolivia $14,316,148 pesos, much of which was spent to import food the country was perfectly capable of producing. La Paz, for example, imported beef, mutton, and potatoes, among other foods. The local producers might deserve protection from cheaper imports, but protective tariffs alone would not necessarily raise the efficiency of the notoriously inefficient latifundos.

Although taking no legal steps to reform the land structures, Belzu never opposed the Indian occupation of their former community lands and the reestablishment of the *ayllu* wherever the *hacendados* had dispossessed the Indian community. Landlords, fearful of the restive Indian masses, found it prudent to move to the safer confines of the cities, thus abandoning their estates, which the Indians promptly occupied. Two major consequences of the de facto land reforms were the greater supplies of food entering the marketplaces and the drop in the price of food. Belzu further delighted the campesinos by relieving them of some taxes.

If rhetoric were the measure of government, Belzu's administration stood as revolutionary. These examples from his public speeches serve as a yardstick:

> Comrades, an insensitive throng of aristocrats has become arbiter of your wealth and your destiny; they exploit you ceaselessly and you do not observe it; they cheat you constantly and you don't sense it; they accumulate huge fortunes with your labor and blood and you are unaware of it. They divide the land, honors, jobs and privileges among themselves, leaving you only misery, disgrace, and work, and you keep quiet. How long will you sleep? Wake up once and for all. The time has come to ask the aristocrats to show their titles and to investigate the basis for private property. Aren't you equal to other Bolivians? Aren't all people equal? Why do only a few enjoy the conditions of intellectual, moral, and material development and not all of you?

> Companions, private property is the principal source of most offenses and crimes in Bolivia; it is the cause of the permanent struggle among Bolivians; it is the basis of our present selfishness eternally condemned by universal morals. No more property! No more property owners! No more inheritances! Down with the aristocrats! Land for everyone; enough of the exploitation of man. . . . Aren't you also Bolivians? Haven't you been born to equality in this privileged land?

> Friends, to use the expression of a great philosopher: private property is the exploitation of the weak by the strong. Private property is the result of chance. Take justice into your own hands and accomplish what the justice of men and of these times has denied you.

For the great mass of dispossessed campesinos, Belzu's heady words did not fall on idle ears. Some seized the estates. Where the landlords resisted, the followers of Belzu attacked and defeated them. Addressing the people of Cochabamba who had resisted the efforts of the old elite to regain power in 1849, Belzu observed,

> *Cholos,* while you are the victims of hunger and misery, your oppressors, those who call themselves gentlemen while exploiting your labor, live in opulence. Everything you see, however,

> belongs to you because it is the fruit of your sweat. The wealth
> of those who consider themselves the aristocracy is robbed
> from you who have created it.

Spurred by such rhetoric, the folk of Cochabamba sacked the homes and shops of the wealthy. Belzu later excused the pillage as "the impartial justice of the people."

The identification of the folk with President Belzu and vice versa established that harmony and integration between caudillo and people that conferred sweeping power on the former. The president cultivated that identification. From the balcony of the presidential palace, Belzu assured his listeners, "I am one of you, poor and humble, a disinherited son of the people. For that reason, the aristocrats and the rich hate me and are ashamed to be under my authority." The president frequently reminded his followers that all power originated in the people who had conferred it on him. He simply acted on behalf of the people and in their interests. A large portion of his message to congress in 1855 discussed the new socioeconomic forces in motion. He reminded the legislature, "Under my auspices new elements of order and preservation have appeared on the political scene. Classes disinherited by the injustice of the times, people bent beneath the weight of our social structures, have arisen from the rubble to take their place among us." Belzu correctly claimed that those new elements supported his government: "The popular masses have made themselves heard and played their role spontaneously; they have put down rebellions and fought for constitutional government. The rise to power of this formidable force is a social reality of undeniable transcendence." Apparently the president appreciated the similar political situation that existed in Argentina until 1852 under Juan Manuel de Rosas. Belzu reversed previous Bolivian policies toward the Argentine leader, and the two populist caudillos maintained cordial relations. One immediate consequence was the expulsion from Bolivia of the Argentine Unitarian exiles.

In the last analysis, Belzu was too Europeanized himself to feel comfortable for long with the "inorganic democracy" that sustained him as a populist caudillo, for he insisted on codifying his government within the confines of a Europeanized constitution. His political reforms and Constitution of 1851 reduced the presidential term to a specific period and prohibited reelection. Elections in 1855, classified by one historian as "the cleanest every held," brought a constitutional end to the Belzu presidency, awarding the office to the president's preferred candidate, but a man unequal to the tumultuous task. In August, at the height of his powers, he stepped down, unwilling to follow the well-established precedent of *"continuismo,"* turned over the presidency to his elected successor, and temporarily left Bolivia. To the Indian masses, he remained their "tata Belzu," friend and protector, whose short, unique government had benefited them.

The Indians had every reason to be apprehensive of the electoral process in which they played no role. With Belzu in Europe, the old elites easily seized power. At the same time, they took possession of the lands they claimed and returned the campesinos to their former subservience. In the years that followed, the Indians often revolted with cries of "Viva Belzu!" on their lips, but as the elites became increasingly integrated into international trade and consequently strengthened, they were not about to repeat the previous political errors that had permitted a Belzu to govern. When the Huaichu Indians of Lake Titicaca rebelled in 1869 to regain communal lands, for example, President Mariano Melgarejo dispatched the army to massacre them.

In a third nation with a large Indian population, Mexico, examples of grass-roots rebellion abounded in the nineteenth century. The major cause of the protracted violence was the conflict between the expanding estate and the defensive Indian communities. The Indians refused to surrender their lands quietly. The Yaquis of Sonora fought bitterly against the central government throughout the nineteenth century. In 1825 the Yaqui leader Juan Banderas cleared the Yaqui Valley of Mexicans as a protest against taxation and alienation of the Indian lands. That conflict between the Yaquis and Mexicans intensified — as it did everywhere — with the arrival of the railroad. Railroad construction in Sonora during the Porfiriato encouraged the expansion of haciendas and mining, economic enterprises that absorbed the Yaquis' land and demanded their labor. They had to acquiesce or to fight. The Yaquis chose to resist. José María Leyva Cajeme organized and governed a Yaqui state-within-a-state from 1875 until his death in 1886. Resistance declined before the overwhelming federal forces,

but a handful of rebels under Juan Maldonado, alias Teta-
biate, raided haciendas, ranches, and mines during the last
decade of the century. The government responded to Yaqui
rebellion by selling the Indians into virtual slavery to the owners of the labor-short henequin plantations in distant Yucatan.

The Sierra Gorda, a region falling within the three states of
Hidalgo, Querétaro, and Guanajuato, seethed with turmoil between 1810 and 1875, following a pattern for that area well
established during the colonial period. The Indians either
fought to defend their lands from the increasing incursions of
whites or to regain lands already lost. In the period 1842-1845,
peasant uprisings swept through southwestern Mexico encom-
passing all or parts of the states of Oaxaca, Guerrero, Puebla,
Morelos, Mexico, and Michoacan. The failures of the Indian
and mestizo peasants in those areas increased the oppression
and misery that had become their lot as the large estates spread
in size and number.

The Tzotzil Maya of Chiapas under the leadership of Pedro
Días Cuscat, 1867-1870, rebelled to restore Indian power to
the Chiapan highlands and thus rescue the community from
mestizo oppression. As one means of creating a new Indian
society and religion and of eradicating mestizo influence, the
Indians sought to create their own Mayan Christ. To do so they
crucified a ten-year-old Indian boy, who was to become a
"new, Indian son of God and Sun/Christ." Bitter ethnic conflict characterized Cuscat's war. Several times the Mayas nearly
toppled the state government in San Cristobal de las Casas
before federal and state troops defeated them.

Meanwhile, Manuel Lozada (1828-1873), son of impoverished peasants, assumed leadership of the Indians against the
hacendados encroaching on their lands in Jalisco (today the
region in which he was most active lies in the newer state of
Nayarit). For years he dominated western Jalisco as the unquestioned *cacique* and champion of Indian rights. From the late
1850s onward, he supported the redivision of lands to favor the
dispossessed rural masses. Finally, in early 1873, he proclaimed
his *Plan Libertador* to institute land reform and proceeded to
carry it out, much to the horror of the elites. The Mexico City
newspaper *El Siglo XX* (Feb. 7, 1873) predicted "social disintegration by attacking the rights of property" and characterized

the actions of Lozada and his followers as "fanatic, ignorant, and nasty barbarism." Fighting against governmental forces in mid-July 1873 he was captured and executed.

Rare were the years in central Mexico without campesino protest, but serious rural uprisings tended to group themselves into particularly chaotic periods: 1832-34, 1842-44, 1847-49, 1855-56, 1868-69, 1878-84, 1986, and 1906. Some kind of record for rural unrest in Mexico was set in the period 1877-1884, which witnessed fifty-five separate incidents of protest. Hacienda and railroad expansions with the resultant incursions into Indian lands ignited nearly every one of them. The Indians rebelled on ten occasions, occupied hacienda lands on four, and engaged in peaceful protests on forty-one. Their restraint was notable in the face of the extreme violence inflicted on them by the hacendados, who used physical dispossession, terror tactics, assassinations, kidnappings, and state and federal troops to gain more lands, to intimidate the Indians, and to terminate the protests.

Doubtless the major Indian rebellion in terms of length, carnage, and significance was the Caste War of Yucatan between the Mayas and the peninsula's whites and mestizos. In the years after Mexico declared its independence, the sugar and henequin plantations had expanded to threaten the corn culture of the Mayas by incorporating their lands into the latifundia and by impressing the Indians into service as debt peons. The Indians fought for their land and freedom. They defended their world. On the other side, the Yucatan elite professed that they fought for "the holy cause of order, humanity, and civilization." Much of the bloodiest fighting occurred during the period 1847-1855, but the war lingered on until the early twentieth century. During those decades the Mayas of eastern and southern Yucatan governed themselves.

Free of white domination, the Mayan rebels took the name of Cruzob, turned their backs on the white world, and developed their own culture, a synthesis of their Mayan inheritance and Spanish influences. Four hundred years of conquest had erased the intellectual and artistic heritage from the Mayan mind, but the Cruzob retained their knowledge of agriculture and village and family organization from the pre-Columbian past. Unique to the Cruzob was the development of their own religion, based largely on their interpretation of Christianity. Unlike other syncretic religions of Latin America, it developed without dependence on the sporadic participation of Roman Catholic priests (to perform baptisms, marriages, or an occasional mass) and free from the critical eye of the white master. Incorporating the Indian folkways, it strengthened the Cruzob and provided a spiritual base for independence other Indians lacked. What was notable about the Cruzob was the emergence of a viable Indian alternative to Europeanization. Although infused with Spanish contributions, it bore a strong resemblance to the pre-Columbian Mayan society. Reviving their Indian culture by repudiating "foreign" domination and substituting their own values for "foreign" ones, the Cruzob revitalized their society. They became masters of their own land again.

Powerful forces at work in the closing decades of the nineteenth century overwhelmed the Cruzob. The poor soil of Yucatan exhausted under corn cultivation no longer yielded sufficient food. Disease reduced the Indian ranks faster than battle did. At the same time, Mexico, increasingly stable under Porfirio Díaz, showed less tolerance for the Cruzob, and more determination to subdue them in order to exploit Yucatan. A treaty between Mexico and Great Britain closed British Honduras to the Cruzob, thus cutting off their single source of modern weapons and ammunition. Finally, the expanding railroads and roads from northern Yucatan accompanying the prosperous henequin plantations penetrated the Cruzob territory. A growing market for forest woods sent the whites even into the seeminly impenetrable forest redoubts of the Cruzob. Consequently a declining Cruzob population and relentless Mexican pressures brought to an end the Mayan independence of half a century. The long and tenacious resistance testified to the Indian preferences, a rejection of the Europeanization preferred by the elites.

In Ecuador, Indian uprisings punctuated the nineteenth century. The Ecuadorian scholar Oswaldo Albornaz P. has chronicled twenty such rebellions caused by increased taxation, harsh exploitation, and a desire to defend or recover communal lands. One of the major rebellions broke out in 1871 in

Chimborazo province, where the Indians sought to end the abuses and crushing taxation of the Garcia Moreno government. The chief of the rebellion, Francisco Daquilema, was condemned to death by a military tribunal and has been banished from "history" by Ecuadorian historians. Peruvian history witnessed similar Indian protest. Overwork, excessive taxation, and general abuse goaded the Indians to rebel in Puno in 1866 and in Ancash in 1885. In the latter uprising the Indians captured the departmental capital, Huaráz, and several other towns before the army dispersed them. The Indian leader Pedro Pablo Atusparia emerged from the struggle as a genuine folk hero revered by his people, although—to repeat a pattern well established by now—ignored by the official histories of Peru. Still, three remarkable intellectuals, Juan Bustamente, Clorinda Matto de Turner, and Manuel González Prada attempted to focus national attention on the plight of the indigenous population. The first was executed; the second sent into exile. In both Argentina and Chile the Indians maintained the resistance they had mounted since the sixteenth century. Benjamín Vicuña Mackenna spoke out in the Chilean parliament on several occasions between 1868 and 1876 to denounce the Indians as "our enemies." Their defense of their lands elicited words such as "cowardly," "rapacious," "usurper," "robber," "fraud" from the historian in his political pronouncements. But neither verbal nor military attacks dislodged the tenacious Araucanians, who managed to hold back the advancing frontiers of the Europeanized estates until the last decades of the century and, in fact, technically neither surrendered nor were defeated.

In those nations where slavery lingered after independence, the blacks vigorously protested their servitude and the institutions that allowed it. They threatened the local slaveholders and intensified the anxieties of the governments. Cirilo Villaverde in his extremely popular novel *Cecilia Valdes* (the definitive edition was published in 1882) depicted the Cuban plantations as a battle field of the races: "There existed a permanent state of war, bloody, cruel, implacable, of black against white, of master against slave." Visions of the successful slave revolt in Haiti haunted the elites just as it inspired slaves. Unrelenting black pressure through guerrilla warfare helped to persuade the Colombian government to manumit the remaining slaves in 1852. Major slave threats to established order occurred in Venezuela in 1835 and Peru in 1848. Brazilian slaves constantly rebelled until final abolition in 1888. In fact, the period just prior to abolition, 1882–1887, witnessed a sharp increase in rebellions, runaways, and assassinations of slave owners. Perhaps the major slave revolt occurred in 1835 in Bahia, scene of nine revolts or attempts since the opening of the century. Well organized and directed by Nagos slaves, the rebels sought to kill all whites and to free all slaves. Though the uprising failed, it sent shivers of fear throughout the white community, which never abated until slavery was abolished. The president of the province of Bahia expressed his opinion that "dangerous and suspicious" freedmen, especially those born in Africa (probably the majority in 1835), who did not share the "language, customs, or even the religion" of the Europeanized Brazilians should not be considered citizens protected by the guarantees of the constitution and should be repatriated.

Sober members of the elites regarded the slave "a volcano that constantly threatens society, a mine ready to explode," as Agostino Marques Perdigão Malheiros phrased it in his authoritative study *A Escravidão no Brazil* (1866). One such slave who did "explode" in violent protest was Lucas da Feira (1807–1849), and his life offers some needed insight into slave rebellion. As a youth he repeatedly fled slavery only to be repeatedly recaptured. At age twenty he escaped his master and lived alone, hiding in the Bahian countryside until 1840, when he joined with other black runaways. Chief of the group until captured and executed, he earned a reputation as a kind of black Robin Hood robbing the rich and sharing his gains with the humble. As one popular verse about his exploits stated, "Poor men I never robbed." More than 150 deaths were attributed to him. Feared by the rich and powerful, he enjoyed the respect of the poor. Of course Brazil's laws and elites judged Feira as a criminal. He, by contrast, viewed himself as the avenger of injustice and degradation, an opinion that other segments of the masses must have shared. Foreign visitors sensed the tensions created by slave society. Prince Adalbert visited one large and well-run plantation, which he praised as a model. After noting the seemingly friendly relations between the master and the slaves, he revealed, "The loaded guns and pistols hanging up in his [the master's] bedroom, however, showed that he had not entire confidence in them [the slaves] and indeed, he had more than once been obliged to face them with his loaded gun." Panama City, particularly, seethed with racial tensions during the decades 1850–1880. The black urban masses resented their depressed conditions using violence—robberies, fires, rioting—as a means of protest. Many referred to the situation as a "race war," exacerbated by an economic reality in which the poor were black and the rich, white.

The blacks mastered satire as one means to relieve their frustrations and express their disdain of the dominant, white elites. In their African languages, the slaves sang lyrics ridiculing their masters. Some of the songs immortalized the resistance of the slaves. One such song from Trinidad of the early 1830s gleefully recorded the inability of the master to prevent the fires set in the cane fields by the runaways. Knowning nothing of the languages, the masters in their naivete sometimes accompanied the music good-naturedly by clapping their hands, nodding, and smiling, much to the added delight of their black detractors.

The story of the slave rebellions and of the reactions of the Latin American blacks to their society in the nineteenth century remains to be told. Although historians take note of some of the blacks' protests against the nineteenth century's most brutal institution, they inevitably credit abolition to one or another enlightened, "Europeanized" president or leader, a gift generously bestowed on grateful blacks, failing to do justice to the struggle of a determined people to win its own freedom.

Novelists, although often sympathetic in their prose to the plight of the blacks, generally failed to depict the reality of being a slave—or, for that matter, a black—in a Europeanized society but did suggest the status of racial relations and a degree of societal violence. In her novel *Sab* (1841), the Cuban Gerturdis Gómez de Avellaneda made the faithful mulatto slave Sab sacrifice the wealth acquired from a winning lottery ticket for his master's family, a symbolic gesture revealing the whites' perception of the blacks' role. To further carry out the symbolism, Carlota, daughter of Sab's master and object of the black's affections, to whom he secretly transferred the lottery ticket, married an English merchant and, although she might not have been happy, she traveled widely, lived well, and apparently fulfilled the island's desire of union with the new metropolis. Later in the century, Aluizio Azevedo related in *O Mulato* (1881) how Raimundo felt as a light-skinned, blue-eyed mulatto in Brazilian society, an exposé of the subtleties of racial prejudice. Sab, the slave, committed suicide, forced to self-destruction by society; Raimundo, the free mulatto, was assassinated, a vengeance society wreaked upon him because he dared to act the equal of the "white" Brazilians. These novelists were recording the observation that free or slave the person of African descent was caught in the maelstrom of violence in nineteenth-century Latin America.

Like the blacks struggling against enslavement or decrying their menial economic positions and the Indians defending their lands, cultures and labor, other popular segments of the varied Latin American populations signified their disagreements with the elitist institutions and the commitment to Europeanize. Indeed, the forms modernization assumed — the expansion of the latifundia oriented toward export, the constructions of railways with the resultant opening to export agriculture of regions once linked with folk societies, the encouragement of European immigration with land grants, the elimination of folk societies and ridicule of folk cultures — ignited protest, rebellion, and sedition throughout the century.

The first half of the nineteenth century marked a notable period of popular unrest, violence, and rebellion in Brazil. It may well be the period of Brazilian history in which the masses expressed most protest and played their most active political role. Large numbers of the popular classes throughout the provinces resented their status and feared the changes imposed on them. Bahia, in particular, during the years 1824–1840, seethed with social protest. In general terms, it is safe to conclude that the Bahian rebels were people of color who opposed or fought against the "European types." Their ideology was vague and often contradictory. They frequently sacked shops and warehouses in a quest for food and killed military officers and landowners in a challenge to authority.

In the 1830s, also, three major popular rebellions revealed the unrest in the northeast and north of Brazil: the War of the

Cabanos in the interior of Pernambuco and Alagoas, 1832-1836; the Cabanagem in Pará, 1835-1840; and the Balaiada in Maranhão, 1838-1841. These three, of the many that rocked the empire in that turbulent decade, appear to have had the most popular support and expressed the frustrations of poor whites, mestizos, mulattoes, black slaves, and Indians. The rebels hoped to improve their standards of living, although their programs were vague, and to share in the exercise of power. The War of the Cabanos was particularly significant because it was entirely rural based. The leader, Vicente Ferreira da Paula, is considered to be an "authentic leader of the masses," according to a revisionist study of the rebellion. The case of da Paula illustrates the thin line that often separated "banditry" from "rebellion." Depending on whose point of view the reader accepts, da Paula has been depicted as both bandit and rebel. Indeed, he undoubtedly played multiple roles, but the point to be emphasized here and later is the frequent merging of bandit and rebel and the facility of transition from one to the other, a facility further accented by vague definitions of each. While leaders of the three rebellions were revered by their followers, who considered them to be one of themselves, the governments branded them "criminals," "bandits," and "outlaws," which they are still termed whenever mentioned in the official histories. For example, in a history text, *História do Brazil* by Hélio Vianna, widely used during the 1960s in Brazilian universities, the author spoke of the Balaiada as "unchecked banditry," and the principal allegation against the rebels is their "audacity to attack private property." The proclamation in 1840 of the young Pedro II to be of age to reign and his subsequent coronation strengthened the control of the elites but did not eliminate displays of popular wrath. Repeated urban riots agitated Recife in 1848, the culmination of previous popular dissatisfaction with high food prices, Portuguese commercial domination, and the arrival of German manual laborers who received jobs the locals needed. The Ronco de Albeha revolt in Paraíba in 1852 and the Movimento dos Marimbondos in Pernambuco at the same time objected to the new law requiring civil registration of birth, a requirement suspected by the people of color as a means to enslave them. As often happened in Latin America, they saw in the Roman Catholic

Church a protector, while they suspected the state of being the exploiter. As a result of the uprisings, church registration continued until 1889, after the abolition of slavery.

Incidents in the Parahyba Valley in the 1850s illustrated social and economic tensions engendered by expanding export agriculture. A booming coffee economy enriched the valley during that decade, and as demand and price rose, the coffee barons scurried to extend their plantings, a move that threatened the small farmers and squatters. Confrontations between the two groups multiplied, but the inexorable inundation of coffee trees swept the less privileged from the cultivation of the land, although not without some damage to local social tranquillity. Other popular manifestations disturbed the order dear to the Brazilian elite: the Carne sem Osso movement in 1858 and the Vintem in 1880.

The Quebra-Quilo Revolt, late 1874 to early 1875, ranked high in significance because the peasants of the interior of the Northeast succeeded in checking the Brazilian government's new modernization drive under way by 1871 but ineffectual by 1875. The causes of the revolt were not unique: new taxes and the threat peasants felt from the large landowners absorbing their farms, complicated by the imposition of the metric system and the required payment of fees for official alteration and authentication of weights. A journalist covering the revolt attributed it to "the direct consequence of the suffering and deprivation . . . [of] the working classes of the interior," while a peasant participant claimed, "The fruit of the soil belongs to the people and tax ought not be paid on it." As riots multiplied in the marketplaces from Rio Grande do Norte to Alagoas, the municipal and provincial authorities feared the "forces of Barbarism" were poised to sweep across the Northeast. The peasants were unusually successful. They did not pay the new taxes; they destroyed the new weights and measures; they burned official records and archives, thus protecting their informal title to the land by reducing to ashes the legal records. In most cases, those peasants had taken physical possession of the land and worked it over the generations without title. They faced possible eviction by anyone who could show the proper paper authenticating legal ownership. By destroying records, the peasants removed evidence—the local notorial registers of land, for example—from use in judicial proceedings, thereby putting themselves on equal legal footing with the local landed elite. Momentarily, then, the sporadic riots that constituted the revolt achieved the peasants' goals, while temporarily frustrating the penetration of the elites into their region.

Popular protests were not unique to Brazil. Throughout South America the common people expressed their disagreement with elitist rule. Beneath the political rebellions troubling Venezuela between 1844 and 1848 swirled currents of rural social unrest, a desire to rectify glaring social injustices. The rural masses abandoned the estates to take up arms, demanding land reform, abolition of slavery, and an end to taxation. Some of the freedmen participating in the insurrections advocated the elimination of the whites from Venezuela, since they associated the oppressive institutions with the European population. Angered by the absorption of their lands by the growing latifundia, armed groups of men circulated through the streets of Cali, Colombia, on the nights of May 20 and 21, 1848, shouting, "Long live the people and death to the whites!" Then they tore down fences erected by two hacendados which had deprived the peasants of pasture for their animals. Governor Vicente Borrero of the province of Buenaventura noted in a letter the following month to President Tomás Cipriano de Mosquera, "The People are constantly at war with the Landowners, and the Landowners with the People." Blood frequently soaked the fertile Cauca Valley. Following the familiar scenario, the landlords sought to expand their holdings and met resistance from threatened peasants as well as from the landless who wanted access to land. Because many of the peasants were black and the landlords white, the struggle in the valley assumed characteristics of racial war. In the six years after Buenos Aires took control of the newly centralized government, 1862–1868, and while President Mitre determined to impose urban, elitist government over folk culture, Argentina witnessed 117 rebellions with ninety-one battles and the deaths of 4,728 citizens. Revolts again shook the province of Santa Fé in 1893. The small farmers protested a tax on wheat to pay for the government's innovations, including railroads, that seemed to favor the large landowners. Furthermore, they resented the fact that immigrants received land and preferred treatment denied the locals. Social disorder rose impressively in the province of Tucumán between 1876 and 1895. During those two decades the number of arrests, ones involving mostly illiterate workers, jumped from under two thousand per year to over seventeen thousand, while the total population only doubled during the same period.

This does not constitute a complete catalog of popular rebellions. It will take long and careful research even to compile a representative sampling, let alone a description and understanding of such protests. The few examples given in this discussion only suggest how the pace of modernization partly accounted for rebellion and its attendant violence in nineteenth-century Latin America. Such rebellions were, despite the silence of conventional historiography, a salient trend of that century.

Popular protest also assumed forms other than rebellion. Banditry and millenarian movements flourished in the nineteenth century, although serious studies of them are still rare. Thanks to the conceptual framework offered by E. J. Hobsbawm, it is possible with many cautions to consider banditry as a form of social protest and millenarianism as a type of popular revolution. It now remains for historians to identify the bandits and the millenarian movements as a first step toward understanding their significance in nineteenth-century Latin America.

Brazil offers numerous examples of both millenarianism and banditry in the past century. Intensifying urbanization, the growth of commercial agriculture, and the expansion of transportation and communication challenged the folkways of the rural population and sparked cultural conflicts. The despair of the rural masses, their rejection of the present, and their longing for a better life in the future, in turn, gave rise to millenarian movements.

In the backlands of Pernambuco, 1817–1820, Silvestre José dos Santos established the City of Heaven on Earth, where his followers expected riches during their temporal life distributed by the mystic sixteenth-century Portuguese monarch Sebastian, the perennial hope of the dispossessed. In 1836–1839 miserably poor people concentrated in Pedra Bonita in the arid interior of Pernambuco to await the metamorphosis of the barren rocks into an enchanted city in which they would enjoy grace, riches, and power, once again through the intervention of King Sebastian. As previously mentioned, Antônio Conselheiro attracted throngs of faithful followers at Canudos, 1893–1897, discouraged with contemporary Brazil and hopeful of improvement. Broadly speaking, Canudos challenged the oppressive institutions that favored the elite. The complex movement in the interior of Ceará associated with Padre Cícero began in 1889, when the host administered by the priest reputedly turned to blood in the mouth of the communicant. The fame and authority of Padre Cícero spread rapidly throughout the Northeast, lasted throughout his lifetime (he died in 1934), and continues to be a force to reckon with in that depressed region. Like Canudos, it reflected both harsh and changing economic realities; it was a movement part spiritual and part practical. Padre Cícero promised a better life for the faithful and worked to ameliorate the misery of his followers. In the extreme south of Brazil, a messianic movement among German immigrants occurred between 1872 and 1898. Jacobina Maurer, the self-proclaimed reincarnation of Jesus Christ, announced the end of the world and life everlasting for her followers. Parenthetically, this movement offers one of the very few examples of female leadership during the nineteenth century. Periodically throughout the century, small messianic movements flourished in the Amazon basin. In the tribes deculturated by missionaries and explorers, the Indians developed a syncretic religion, part Roman Catholic, part that of their ancestors. They turned to that religion for unity and hope. Messianic movements flourished which denounced "white civilization" as the source of local misery and announced a new and perfect life in which the whites would not be present. The masses often conceived of the millennium as a world without whites, whom they universally equated with exploitation and associated with their misery.

Such messianic movements flourished among the Andean Indians since conquest. They yearned for a return to the order, basically Incan, destroyed by the Spanish conquest, one which would benefit them rather than the outsider. Exemplary of such movements was the one that occurred among the Bolivian Indians of Curuyaqui in 1891–92. An individual called Tumpa and known as "the superior being" appeared in the community announcing his mission "to liberate them from the whites."

"My kingdom is not of this world," he advised his adherents. Under the new system, Tumpa promised that the whites would work for the Indians. His followers took up arms as urged by their messianic leader; the whites fled to the cities; and the army arrived to brutally crush the uprising. The carnage disproved at least two of Tumpa's prophecies: first that only water would issue forth from the soldiers' guns and second that anyone who did die for the cause would return to life in three days.

The wheat-growing center of Tandil in southern Buenos Aires province (quite removed culturally and geographically from the Amazon and Andes), was another scene of a millenarian movement with related goals. Immigrants amassed the land and reduced the gauchos to underpaid laborers. Psychologically those dispossessed gauchos were ready to accept the *curandero* and religious figure Gerónimo G. de Solané, widely called Tata-Dios, when he arrived in Tandil in 1871 preaching the millenium. He informed his ready adherents that salvation would be achieved by murdering the hated foreigners. Under his leadership, a group of gauchos killed thirty people on New Year's Day, 1872, far short of their goal of eliminating all foreigners, before the police could intervene to stop them.

Northwestern Mexico was the scene of the miracle cures of Teresa Urrera (1873–1903), referred to by hundreds of thousands of devotees as Teresita or the Saint of Cabora. In 1889 after a severe psychological shock, she lapsed into a comatose state. Considered dead, she regained life just prior to her burial. She reported having spoken to the Blessed Virgin, who conferred on her the power to cure. By 1891, pilgrims flooded Cabora seeking her help, Teresita's compassion for the poor earned her the devotion of the masses and the suspicion of the Díaz government. The Yaquis and Mayos confided in her and unburdened their sufferings before her. Believing she enjoyed influence with God, they pressed her for help and advice. In 1890 the Tarahumara Indian mountain village of Tomochic adopted Teresita as their saint, placing a statue of her in their church. The village began to modify its Roman Catholicism to a more indigenous one focused on the Saint of Cabora. The next year Tomochic rebelled against the government and requested Teresita to interpret God's will to them. The government reaction was immediate and harsh, but it still took several armed expeditions to quell the rebellion. The village was destroyed, and not a man or boy over thirteen years of age survived the slaughter. In mid-May of 1892 a group of approximately two hundred Mayo Indians led by Juan Tebas and Miguel Terigogui attacked the town of Navojoa shouting, "Viva la Santa de Cabora!" Considering her a dangerous agitator of the masses, the Días government exiled Teresa Urrea to the United States. Even from the other side of the border her influence was felt. In 1896 a group of Yaqui Indians crossed the border into Mexico attacking government garrisons and shouting "Viva Santa Tereza!" Teresita, herself opposed to violence, had served more as a figurehead, a catalyst, a remarkable charismatic personality whose compassion gave unity of expression to the miserable masses of Northwestern Mexico.

Similar to the folk cultures already discussed, the millenarian movements evinced a strict hierarchy of authority in which the acknowledged leader ruled supremely and — it was assumed — always in the best interests of the people. Much research will have to be completed before we can conclude whether millenarianism, so pervasive in the nineteenth century, was any more common in the century after independence than it had been during the colonial centuries. Its characteristics seem similar in both periods for understandable reasons. It continued to be a manifestation of cultural conflict and the tensions of acculturation, the former well illustrated by the Amazonean examples and by Tata-Dios in Argentina, while Padre Cícero and Jacobina Maurer represented the latter. These millenarian movements revealed both the spiritual and temporal needs of the people who subscribed to them, a denunciation of the society in which they dwelled and a longing for a better life.

Banditry attracted the desperate, those who had lost out in the system whether they were the poor or members of the impoverished gentry. Whatever else banditry might have included or meant, it also was a means of protesting an injustice or righting a wrong as it was of equalizing the wealth or taking political revenge. Although unsympathetic to banditry, the Brazilian jurist of the midnineteenth century Tavares Bastos realized the bandits were victims of the state who, no longer confiding in its laws, made their own justice. The president of the province of Alagoas, however, had harsher words for them in 1833: "Men more like cannibals than citizens, without principals, morals, and religion, they imitate the wild beasts." He invoked the ubiquitous civilization/barbarism theme. To the rich and powerful, bandits were outlaws meriting severe punishment; to the poor masses, however, they often represented justice and liberation.

Bandits roamed the Brazilian interior in the nineteenth century, particularly the impoverished Northeast, where many won the admiration of the poor and the respect of the wealthy, who not infrequently coopted them and utilized their services. Some scholarship correlates the rise of banditry in the late nineteenth century with the breakdown of patriarchal order in the countryside. Brazilian popular poetry abounds with tales of the bandit hero. A well-known one, sung at the beginning of the twentieth century, related the history of Antônio Silvino (1875- 1944), who became a "cangaceiro" in 1896 to avenge an injustice: his father was slain by a police official who went unpunished by the government. Others relate the adventures of Josuíno Brilhante (1844-1879), also seemingly pushed into banditry to avenge injustices against his family. He assaulted the rich and distributed their goods and money among the poor, boasting that he never robbed for himself. Such robberies and redistributions of wealth received the disapprobation of the newspaper *O Cearense,* which in 1878 huffed, "These bandits loot properties in the most unrestricted fashion as if communism had already been proclaimed among us."

Banditry characterized much of Spanish Latin America as well. Mexican banditry flourished, and interestingly enough regions that produced bandits, such as Chalco-Rio Frío, eastern Morelos, and northwestern Puebla, spawned agrarian revolutionaries before the century ended, providing further evidence of the social dimension banditry could assume on occasion. Peru offers numerous examples of peasant bandits. In his study of Peruvian banditry, Enrique López Albujar described it as "a protest, a rebellion, a deviation, or a simple means of subsistence." He concluded that nineteenth-century Peruvian banditry produced folk heroes like Palomo, Pajarito, Sambambé, and Luis Pardo because those bandits corrected injustices, robbed to help the poor, and protested social and economic inequalities, social objectives he did not find prevalent in twentieth-century banditry. Bandits roamed Chile in the first half of the century, but in the last half were confined largely to the southern regions where their activities often were identified or confused with aspects of the bitter warfare between the government and the Indians. Chilean officials lumped together bandits and Indians of the rugged Andes as "criminals." They also routinely complained that local populations, the poor and some of the more affluent farmers as well, supported the bandits, thus facilitating their anti-establishment activities.

Bandits abounded in Spanish American literature, populating the pages of novels and short stories written both in the last century and in the present. Ignacio Manuel Altamirano provided both a critical and sympathetic account of the protagonist in *El Zarco, the Bandit* (written in 1888 but published in 1901). Eloping with El Zarco in the final pages of the novel, Manuela accepted a not unusual rationalization for banditry, "That El Zarco and his followers were bandits—men who had made robbery and kidnapping their profession—did not seem particularly strange to her, for political leaders in revolt against the government often used the same methods. To her, the bandits were rebels at war with society, their cruelty a natural reaction of a life of constant danger." Indeed, Altamirano had already informed his readers that El Zarco had become a bandit after "tiring of a life of servitude and poverty." In short, banditry became a means of protest against social and economic injustice. Similarly in an early Guatemalan novella, "Recuerdos de Copán Calé" (1862), the author took an understanding and sympathetic view of a bandit. Falling into the hands of Monreal, widely feared as the most infamous bandit of Central America, the narrator found him to be "courteous and decent," an intelligent individual. Significantly in this story, Monreal revealed to the narrator the glories of Guatemala's Indian past by taking him to a lost Mayan city. The literary bandits incarnated idealizations of one sort or another, the recognition by one group of intellectuals of just causes for dissatisfaction among larger segments of the population. In ascribing a nobility to the bandits, they implied a need for social reforms. The real bandits probably revealed a character more harmonious with desperation. Their motives and activities varied widely, but at least in part they could be explained as protests against the wrongs of society, as they viewed it.

Because of their strength and because they often opposed the elites and official institutions, they received the support, indeed the admiration of large numbers of the humble classes who often hid them, lied to the authorities to protect them, guided them through strange terrain, and fed them. To the poor, they were caudillos who by default helped to sustain the folk cultures.

Of the varied alternatives offered to the Westernization imposed by the urban elites, few at this point in research seem clear in either their goals or their methods. Thus far, they emerge most notably as protests, expressions of dissatisfaction with urban growth, exotic ideas and customs, foreign presence, higher taxes, forced labor, vaccination, loss of land, and affronts to local traditions. New insight will be required before authoritative conclusions can be drawn from nineteenth-century popular protests. For the present, one can only speculate that larger numbers of Latin Americans, probably the majority, seemed to prefer their folk cultures. Some of the rural patriarchs concurred with popular sentiments, but their reasoning may have included a reluctance to disturb their comfortable position as much as a loyalty to the past. The popular rebellions, protests, banditry, and millenarianism, albeit diverse in their Latin American manifestations over the course of a century, traced most of their roots to folk culture. The folk by no means rejected change in order to preserve the past unaltered. Rather, they would mediate change over a longer period of time. The folk—and a portion of the elites—refused to denounce their Ibero-Afro-Indian heritage in order to import indiscrminately ideas, artifacts, and life-styles of Northern Europe and the United States. The Indians, not surprisingly, looked to their own rich past with its well-defined customs, languages, and relationships; still, they recognized the input of the conquerors' innovations. The Cruzob, for example, embraced cultural patterns that did not replicate their Mayan forebears but rather demonstrated a pragmatic blend of cultures confected by centuries of exposure to European institutions. Vague as the concept of "inorganic democracy" might appear in retrospect, it did hold meaning to the gauchos who identified it with their life-styles, a unique adaptation of limited aspects of European civilization to the demands of the pampas. Their successful adaptation to their environment was their best resistance for a long time to a determined Europeanization of Argentina fostered by the elites of Buenos Aires. The folk societies varied. Yet, they all managed to provide their members with land, to assure that all had work, housing, food, and care, to mediate disputes, and to encourage harmony. Whether they afforded the most comfortable and satisfactory life-styles can be debated, but we know, thanks to historical hindsight, that for the masses no better alternative to those folk societies existed in the nineteenth century.

Doubtless the most successful resistance to Europeanization took place in Paraguay where, during the decades from 1810 to 1870, a native alternative took form, influenced in almost equal parts by the American and European past. Since Paraguay challenged the trend toward wholesale Westernization more effectively than any other group or nation, it merits, as a form of conclusion, special attention. Three caudillos dominated Paraguay in the 1810-1870 period: José Gaspar Rodríguez de Francia (1814-1840), Antonio Carlos López (1840- 1863), and Francisco Solano López (1863-1870).

Francia charted the course for Paraguay's autonomous revolution, which ensured national sovereignty, economic independence, and possibly the only example of economic development in ninetenth-century Latin America. A scrupulously honest lawyer, who prior to his elevation as chief of the nation, customarily had defended the poor and weak in the courts, Francia became closely identified with the expression and execution of the popular will. With only minimal contacts with the outside world, the landlocked nation under his leadership emerged as the most egalitarian society yet known in the Western Hemisphere. He accomplished this unique development by eliminating from power several mighty groups whose governments in the rest of Latin America perpetuated the area's economic dependency. Francia nationalized the Roman Catholic church, confiscating its temporal goods, abolishing the tithe, and decreeing religious freedom. Thus, he not only eliminated a potential rival but avoided the church-state conflicts that eroded national harmony throughout most of Latin America. He removed the traditional, although small and modest, elites from power and destroyed their base of prestige and wealth by nationalizing most of their estates. In possession of the majority of the nation's land, the government established scores of prosperous state ranches and rented the rest for a nominal fee to anyone willing to till the soil or use the land for pasturage. No latifundia dominated the economy, nor did monocultural export deform it. Paraguay became self-sufficient in the production of food, offering the unique example of governmental control of the land for the benefit of society. While the establishment of a state ironworks and state textile and livestock industries provided employment for thousands of Paraguayans, small handicraft industries further augmented national production, thereby meeting the simple, basic needs of the people. Through a rigidly enforced system of trade licenses and its own massive participation, the state prevented the growth of a native or foreign commercial class; no foreign interests were permitted to penetrate the economy; nor did foreign debts, loans, or interest rates hobble it. Francia regulated commerce and controlled the economy to achieve national goals rather than to permit a small group to satisfy individual desires. New information indicates that a rudimentary educational system, satisfactory for the needs of a simple agrarian society, practically eliminated illiteracy.

Continuing on that autonomous and populist course in the three decades after Francia's death, the two Lópezes, father and son, saw to it that Paraguay not only constructed its own modern steamship navy to ply its abundant waterways, built a railroad, and strung telegraph lines, but it also put into operation Latin America's first iron foundry. The two caudillos achieved these innovations without incurring foreign debt and for the benefit of the majority of the Paraguayans. Thereby, Paraguay continued to enjoy economic as well as political independence, escaping the neocolonial dependency characteristic of nineteenth-century Latin America.

The rapid and genuine development of Paraguay under its own form of "inorganic democracy" alarmed the elitist governments in neighboring states, whose own export-oriented economies had grown but failed to develop. They accused Paraguay of upsetting the balance of power in the Rio de la Plata. More realistically, they feared the appealing example Paraguay offered to wider segments of their own population. Argentina,

Brazil, and their puppet-state Uruguay joined forces in the War of the Triple Alliance to bring "civilization" to "barbarian" Paraguay (1864–1870). The Paraguayan masses proved their devotion to their caudillo by fighting tenaciously against their huge neighbors and keeping at bay armies many times their size for over five years. No one has related more poignantly the fanatical defense of Paraguay by its men, women, and children than Juan E. O'Leary in his *Libro de los Heroes* (1922). Financed in part by English loans, the allies waged a war that killed approximately 90 percent of the nation's adult male population. Ironically, the distant *Manchester Guardian* (April 14, 1870), a newspaper that not infrequently voiced the views of expansionist capitalism, pronounced a fitting eulogy for autonomous Paraguay:

> [The war] made a profounder impression on the minds of competent observers than any other conflict. It has destroyed a remarkable system of government. It has overturned the only South American state wherein the native Indian race showed any present likelihood of attaining or recovering such strength or organization as to fit it for the task of government. No other state in South America has been able to boast of so much internal peace.

That English eulogy contrasted with the assessment of the victorious allies.

The Brazilians, who had enjoyed an unusual degree of success in the Plata region overthrowing Uruguayan and Argentine governments, felt satisfaction with their most recent victory in Paraguay, costly as it might have been. Indeed, the Liberal politician and intellectual Tavares Bastos boasted that Brazil once again had opened the door of the Plata to "progress":

> At this happy moment the roar of Brazilian cannons at Humaitá announces to the world that a barbarian government has fallen before our strength, that our gold and green flag fluttering among the banners of our brave allies carries the message of peaceful progress to the isolated villages of Paraguay as it once carried a similar message to the United Provinces of the Rio de la Plata. One after another, first Rosas and now López, falls before free peoples. Our forebears, heralds of the liberal tradition that they initiated in South America, would tremble with joy to see the generous use we make of our power.

The United States minister to Brazil, Henry T. Blow, may never have heard the words of Tavares Bastos, but he instinctively shared the ideas they imparted. At the close of the war he congratulated the Brazilian minister of foreign affairs on the victory of the Triple Alliance, which he equated with the "triumph of civilization."

During the five years of occupation following the war, the allies dismantled the popular institutions of Paraguay's autonomous revolution. They opened the nation to foreign capital and attendant debt. The land passed from the hands of the state and the peasants into huge and unused or underused estates typical of the land patterns of the rest of Latin America. Foreign speculators snapped up land after 1870 at bargain prices. A contemporary French geographer, commenting on postwar Paraguay, singled out the alienation of the land as one of the major new characteristics of the economy. Eliseo Ruclus concluded, "In a few years the vast terrains had been appropriated by absentee landlords; moreover, no campesino could till the soil of his own country without paying rent to the bankers of London, New York, or Amsterdam." Paraguay's alternative to Europeanization ended forcefully in 1870, and thereafter the standard mold of nineteenth-century Latin American institutions characterized that riparian nation.

The Paraguayan experiment is of considerable interest in the study of nineteenth-century Latin America. It existed long enough, more than half a century, to offer a viable alternative to the standard fare of Europeanization with its cosmetic modernization and pervasive and deepening dependency. It provided the best example of what could have or might have occurred had local traditions and preferences won in the intense cultural clash that convulsed Latin America. It offered an example of folk society absorbing and implementing selected aspects of European technology for the benefit of the folk. Thus, it represented a viable alternative to the dichotomy of either folk society or Europeanization. Finally, it established one cogent equation between "inorganic democracy" and the well-being of the folk.

CHAPTER SEVEN

The Poverty of Progress

Westernization triumphed over folk cultures. By the close of the nineteenth century, the Latin American nations had acquired a veneer of progress. The number and mileage of railroad lines expanded; the ports boasted the newest equipment; telegraph and telephone wires reached an ever larger number of cities and towns. An incipient industrialization was under way, and the cities stood on the threshold of a major population explosion. Within those cities an emerging middle class had begun to formulate its goals: primarily an upward mobility more attuned to the life-style of the urban elites than critical of it. The middle class in fact accepted the basic structural and institutional fabric of the nation so long as its members too could clothe themselves in it. The ambitious favored an acceleration of education, industrialization, and a type of nationalism that ensured some job preference for them over foreigners. They regarded those programs as avenues to social mobility, the roads by which they could achieve the life-style they desired. The elites and the middle class strengthened the intellectual, cultural, financial, commercial, and social links with Europe and the United States, whose values they increasingly accepted. They congratulated themselves—and most foreign visitors concurred—on the apparent transformation of Latin America. They judged that their nations were at last on the proper road to progress. Even that superficial modernization helped to fatten public coffers from time to time and brought some financial gains to the elites and middle class. Their lives materially enriched, they concluded, based on their immediate experience, that modernization benefited all. However, that coin of prosperity also revealed another side.

Probably the economic growth of parts of Latin America in the nineteenth century has been overemphasized, even exaggerated. Growth is simply numerical accumulation. Economic growth tells us that something within the economy, or perhaps the economy as a whole, has increased in size. The term alone does not specify what precisely has increased. Was it beans for the masses, the amount of beef exported, or profits for foreign investors? Nor do growth figures customarily reveal who benefited from the growth, although use of per capita figures, so long as they increase, seems to imply that everyone might have. But the growth figures for the nineteenth century had other weaknesses in addition to the facts that they often did not reveal what grew nor explained the significance of a particular growth and, not least of all, that they were frequently inaccurate and inconsistent. They sometimes did not take inflation into account. They often failed to consider the population increases of the same period, from roughly twenty million in 1800 to approximately sixty million in 1900, which put into some question, or at least into a different perspective, the oft-quoted production and income figures as indicators of growth. Growth, when applied to an economy, is a crude standard of judgment, and thus far in studies of nineteenth-century Latin America has infused more confusion than clarification into discussions.

The revisionist studies of nineteenth-century Latin American economic history reflect caution when discussing growth, a sharp contrast with the exuberance of earlier scholarship. Among other things, they are beginning to question the extent of that growth. Nathaniel H. Leff, who has concentrated on nineteenth-century Brazilian economic history, brings into question the conclusion long posited by Celso Furtado and other recognized economists that Brazil experienced a phenomenal growth record in the past century. Instead, Leff talks of "the Brazilian economy's relatively modest growth performance during much of the nineteenth century." The economic growth tended to be confined to the southeastern coffee region; other regions, notably the northeast, witnessed economic declines. As a result, he concluded, "Brazil did not experience a substantial increase in aggregate per capita income during the nineteenth century." The economic portrait of Mexico during the Porfiriato drawn by Charles F. Cumberland was drab, a sober contrast to the panegyrics of those who regarded Díaz and his positivist advisers as economic wizards. For Colombia, William Paul McGreevey pointed to "a reversal in the slow growth of Colombia's economy," and he offered a carefully constructed analysis of that economic "decline" during the last half of the century. Obviously we need to reflect further whether rising exports really indicate a growing economy or only reveal the growth of one sector of the economy counterbalanced perhaps by declines elsewhere.

If some revisionists question the extent of economic growth, others dispute the efficacy of modernization. They seem to suggest that sometimes modernization caused more harm than good. A European-oriented export economy disrupted the Indian and peasant agriculture based on producing food for local consumption. True, the Europeans introduced new crops, trees, and animals, as well as steel and iron tools. Those contributions might have increased production, although the extent of that increase on a per capita rather than an absolute basis remains open to questioning. Further, one must keep in mind that after the European conquest human and geographical resources in the Americas were used increasingly for export products and consequently produced less for local and regional markets. The European-introduced export economy also threatened an ecological and agrarian system that once had sustained at least three huge empires based on food surpluses. José Carlos Mariátegui rated Incan agricultural practices above those introduced by the European: "In Peru, communal property does not represent a primitive economy that has generally been replaced by a progressive economy founded on individual property. No; the 'communities' have been dispossessed of their land for the benefit of the feudal or semifeudal latifundium, which is constitutionally incapable of technical progress." The Europeans commercialized agriculture and drove up food prices in the local market places. Often in the past centuries, the Europeans after arriving in the New World observed techniques that they judged backward and in need of change, only to discover later—at great expense to

themselves, the ecology, and the Latin American economy—
that what at first glance appeared ridiculous to the outsider ensured in the long run the best use of local resources. Much of
the traditional agriculture was ecologically sound. It often constituted a long-evolved adaptation to local conditions and complex rhythms of the local ecosystem. Such a conclusion would
be difficult to apply to most export monoculture. After all, the
coffee plantations virtually desolated the soil of southeastern
Brazil. Any assessment of the benefits of a growing agrarian export economy should question first whether sufficient food was
being produced for local consumption, and second whether the
income earned from the exports contributed to a better quality
of life for the majority.

Further, the revisionists blame modernization for strengthening the negative aspects of some fundamental institutions
inherited from the colonial past, such as the latifundia with its
monoculture, labor exploitation, and socioeconomic privileges
for the landowners. No example better illustrated progress but-
tressing those negative aspects than railroads. It was ironic.
The Latin American elite considered railroads as evidence par
excellence of modernization. Their capitalism mentors had pi-
oneered in railroad construction; European and North American prosperity seemed attributable at least in part to fast,
efficient, low-cost transportation linking raw products, fac-
tories, and consumers into a tight market network. Their intellectual mentors—Comte as well as Spencer—decreed railroads
as essential for progress. Yet, when built in Latin America, the
railroads had just the opposite effects they were expected to
have.

A chief explanation for the strengthening of the colonial institutions by the railroads lies in the fact that more often than
not foreigners built and owned them, and did so where they
would best complement the North Atlantic economies rather
than Latin America's. In Argentina, as but one example,
English-financed, built, equipped, and administered railroads
carried the resources of the rich pampas to the port of Buenos
Aires for their inevitable export. As this example aptly suggests, the railroads served export markets by lowering transportation costs of bulky items, incorporation new regions into
commercial agriculture, and opening up new lands and mines

to exploitation. More often than not, the railroads expanded and strengthened the latifundia wherever the rails reached, since they often conferred considerable value on lands once considered marginal. Whereas previously peasants had been tolerated on that marginal land, its new value caused the landlords first to push the peasants off the land and then to incorporate them into the estate's labor force. Commercial agriculture, much of it destined for export, replaced subsistence agriculture and the numbers and size of the holdings of the small landowners declined. Indian landholdings in particular suffered incursions in those areas touched by the railroads. Mexico proved perfectly the equation of railroad expansion to increased exports, growth of the latifundia, and diminution of small farms. Rail laying in Mexico between 1876 and 1910 pushed the number of miles of tracks from 400 to 15,000. During the same period, exports rose eight and one-half times. John Coatsworth, who studied the effects of rapid railroad expansion between 1877 and 1884 in Mexico, linked that expansion with the burgeoning of the large estate and the transformation of Indian peasants into hired hands, migrant labor, and a kind of rural semiproletariat. He concluded, "If the results of this study may be extended somewhat, they suggest that foreign enterprise in the form of major railroad construction projects significantly altered the shape and balance of Mexico's agrarian system in the last quarter of the nineteenth century." The plantation and mine to port pattern of Latin American railroad construction did little to provide political integration, to serve local, regional, or national markets, and to encourage industrialization. Rather, it further integrated and subordinated Latin America within the North American economy.

Bolivia provides a sobering example of the contribution of railroads both to dependency on a single export and to the destruction of food production for local markets. By the end of the nineteenth century, rails connecting the altiplano with Pacific ports accelerated tin ore exports. The rail cars descended the Andes loaded with the ore. In order to fill the otherwise empty cars on their return, the trains carried agricultural products imported from Peru, Chile, and the United States. The importation of food wrought havoc with the agrarian economy of Santa Cruz, depriving it of its national market.

Production declined sharply. Bolivia became locked into a double dependency status: dependent on foreign markets for its single export and on foreign producers for a part of its food supply.

Costa Rica illustrates in a slightly different, but even more disastrous way the effects of railroads on the economy of a small nation. In the case of Costa Rica, the pursuit of modernization allowed foreigners to take control of the national economy. To market larger quantities of coffee and thus earn the money to modernize, the government encouraged the construction of a railroad during the period 1870–1890 from the highlands where the coffee grew to Puerto Limón for shipment abroad. The onerous loans overburdened the treasury as the government paid usurious interest rates to unscrupulous foreign moneylenders. Further, the government bestowed on Minor Keith, the chief engineer, 800,000 acres, land that fronted on the railroad and later became the center of the plantations of the United Fruit Company. Even so, the railroad remained in foreign hands. British investors also controlled the ports, mines, electric lighting, major public works, and foreign commerce as well as the principal domestic marketplaces. In short, Costa Rica surrendered all its economic independence and mortgaged its future before 1890 in order to attain the accoutrements of modernization. No evidence exists that any Costa Ricans except a tiny elite benefited.

Modernization encouraged foreign investment, and everywhere those outsiders bought up land. The trend throughout the century was for foreign ownership of land to increase, more often than not at the expense of peasant and Indian communities. By 1910, foreigners owned about one-seventh of the total land area of Mexico; by 1914, approximately 40 percent of Argentine farms were in the hands of foreigners. They were almost exclusively interested in producing for the export market.

Investment conferred considerable political influence on the investor. In some cases, the influence was delicately applied; in others it was brutally enforced. The New York and Honduras Rosario Mining Company in the last two decades of the century bent the Honduran government to its will. Local interests took second position to those of the Rosario Mining Company. The presidents moved according to the strings pulled by the company's lawyers and managers. President Luís Bográn (1883-1892) repeatedly acted for the company's best interest. On one occasion he overturned a supreme court decision in order to favor the company and finally decreed the foreign company outside the pale of Honduran courts. Despite all the favoritism bestowed on the company by the government, Honduras benefited little, if at all, from its operations.

Finally, the question of the direction of capital flow awaits more authoritative research. While it is true that large sums of investment capital and loans entered Latin America from the North Atlantic nations and were basic to the shaping of local economies, it is equally true that large amounts of money flowed in the opposite direction as profits and interest rates. Nor should one forget the sums spent by the elites, and to a lesser degree by the middle class, on luxury consumer goods generously imported, investments made and bank accounts kept abroad, and the costs of lavish trips to and extended residencies in Europe. More than a little evidence exists to suggest that the net capital flow probably favored the North Atlantic nations.

Against the claims of the elites to have encouraged growth, fostered progress, and initiated modernization, must be weighed their policies that strengthened colonial institutions, the export-oriented economies, and pervasive foreign control. The balance tipped negatively. Indeed, one major accumulative consequence of the elitist policy was to deepen Latin America's dependency. The Latin American governments were unable to make most of the fundamental decisions that could command the present and shape the future. The economic and political policies imposed by outside capital investment and foreign governments but acquiesced in or willfully encouraged by the elites debilitated Latin America.

Even the largest, the most stable, and the potentially wealthy countries saw their control over their own economies dissipate. Chile was widely regarded by the other Latin Americans to have one of the most stable and most sophisticated of governments. Yet Chile did not prove immune to the devastating effects of modernization financed and directed from abroad. Modernization contributed to change a relatively balanced export economy into one dependent on the sale of a single natural product. Throughout the first three-quarters of the nineteenth century, Chile exported both agricultural goods and minerals. In the 1845–1850 period, agriculture accounted for 45 percent of total exports, while silver, gold, and copper accounted for most of the rest. By the opening of the decade of the 1880s that balance had disappeared. Due to the upsurge in nitrate production, mining represented 78 percent of the exports in 1881. Thereafter, Chile depended heavily on the export of one mineral, first nitrates and then copper, for its export earnings. The building of railroads, the improvement of machinery and technology, the invitations to foreign exports, the increase in foreign investment, all encouraged modernization but also contributed to the concentration on mineral exports. Parallel to increasing dependency on nitrates and copper, Chile witnessed the reduction of its merchant fleet from 276 to 21 ships, and its copper smelters from 250 to 69. The foreigners preferred to use their own ships and to smelt the copper abroad, a preference that could only intensify Chile's dependency. In the last analysis, the new railroads, ports, steamships, technical aid, and loans tied and subordinated the Latin American economy to those of England and the United States, and to a lesser degree to France and Germany.

The differing views of the results of foreign investment in the nineteenth century were well summarized by two opposing Argentine politicians. General Julio A. Roca, first active in the conquest of Indian lands and later twice the president of Argentina, bespoke his gratitude to English investors in a speech in London following a banquet offered in his honor by the investment house of Baring Brothers, a firm extremely influential in the economic destinies of nineteenth-century Latin America:

> I have always had the greatest affection for England. The Argentine Republic, which will one day be a great nation, will never forget that its present state of progress and prosperity is due, in great part, to English capital, which does not fear distance and which has flowed into Argentina in substantial quantities in the form of railroads, streetcar lines, settlements of colonists, the exploitation of minerals, and various other enterprises.

His remarks illustrated the ideology of the Argentine government after the overthrow of Rosas, when the elites succeeded in linking their nation's destiny with that of Europe. Taking another view, the founder of the Socialist Party in Argentina, Juan Bautista Justo, questioned the effects—if not the benefits—of English investments. He wrote in 1896:

> English capital has done what their armies could not do. Today our country is a tributary to England. . . . No one can deny the benefits that the railroads, the gas plants, the streetcars . . . have brought us. But the gold that the English capitalists take out of Argentina, or carry off in the form of products, does us no more good than the Irish got from the revenues that the English lords took out of Ireland. . . . We also suffer from absentee capital. . . . It is that capital that largely prevents us from having sound money and obliges our financial market to submit to a continuous drain of hard currency.

Justo lamented the steady flow of profits and interest payments abroad, but he also recognized and lamented Argentina's surrender of sovereignty. With the immense power over what to loan, to whom, and for what purposes, the English capitalists shaped Argentina's economy—and politics. For Argentina to attract loans and investments, the elites understood they had to guarantee order, stability, peace, and unfettered capitalism. They had to defer to European standards and judgments. Not surprisingly, the European capitalists made their decisions to best suit their own needs with little or no concern for the development of the nations in which they invested, Argentina or any other.

To the degree the Latin American governing elites accepted the decision-making role of the Europeans, they surrendered the independence of their new nations. The resulting dependency made them colonies in all but name. In a comparison of the relations of Great Britain with Uruguay and New Zealand in the nineteenth century, Robin W. Winks concluded that the South American nation was as much a colony of the English as New Zealand. Uruguay was no exception. So large, populous, and potentially wealthy a country as Brazil was completely under the economic sway of the British, who, following a familiar pattern, controlled the export sector of the economy, imports, the railroads, ports, and finances. The extent of that foreign control angered many Brazilian intellectuals. Graça

Aranha analyzed Brazil's dependency in his provocative novel
Canaã ("Canaan", 1902). He concluded that Brazil was a colony of the Europeans:

> "You gentlemen speak of independence," observed the
> municipal judge caustically, "but I don't see it. Brazil is, and
> has always been, a colony. Our regime is not a free one. We
> are a protectorate."
>
> "And who protects us?" interrupted Brederodes, gesticu-
> lating with his monocle.
>
> "Wait a minute, man. Listen. Tell me: where is our finan-
> cial independence? What is the real money that dominates us?
> Where is our gold? What is the use of our miserable paper cur-
> rency if it isn't to buy English pounds? Where is our public
> property? What little we have is mortgaged. The customs
> revenues are in the hands of the English. We have no ships.
> We have no railroads, either; they are all in the hands of the
> foreigners. Is it, or is it not, a colonial regime disguised with
> the name of a free nation. . . . Listen. You don't believe me. I
> would like to be able to preserve our moral and intellectual
> patrimony, our language, but rather than continue this pov-
> erty, this turpitude at which we have arrived, it is better for
> one of Rothschild's bookkeepers to manage our financial af-
> fairs and for a German colonel to set things in order."

That dependency discomforted some intellectuals. It proved
disastrous, however, for the masses.

If claims of economic growth and improvements through
modernization have come under sharper scrutiny, the question
of development has not yet received the attention it deserves.
Development is the utilization of any nation's potential for the
greatest benefit of the largest number of the inhabitants and
must be rigorously differentiated from growth and modernization. Development might further be differentiated from growth
by its concern with consumption levels, rather than the traditional emphasis on production. Who consumes what and how
much become primary questions, a social concern missing from
discussions of growth, where interest focuses exclusively on
statistical evidence of how much is produced. Obviously a
nation can undergo both growth and modernization without
developing. The accumulation of the accoutrements of
modernization certainly does not make a modern nation and

most emphatically does not guarantee development. More often than not, the elites willfully or innocently confused development with growth or even with the superficial modernization they imported, a not uncommon confusion that still characterizes studies of Latin America. Some growth in restricted areas occurred; obviously some modernization did too. However, scant evidence exists that development took place in nineteenth-century Latin America. The elite's devotion to Europe in the last analysis subjected Latin America's well-being to that of its distant mentor, an economic dependency that entailed political subordination, cultural imitation, and social inequity. The elites impoverished Latin America as well as mortgaging its future. It seems reasonable to conclude from the mounting evidence at hand that the progress pursued by the elites was not in the best interests of the masses or, if you will, of development.

The cynical observer might ask whether the elites really wanted more than cosmetic modernization, whether they feared development. Seemingly caught in the web of their own inconsistency, they could not achieve real or meaningful modernization because they refused to reform the inherited colonial institutions. We are left without evidence of any modernization that might have ameliorated the lot of the impoverished majority. Although schools increased in number to accommodate the children of the middle class, they rarely enrolled the children of the masses to prepare them for modernization. Even for the elites, the educational system failed to recognize new realities. The universities continued to emphasize law and theoretical medicine, neglecting the engineering, scientific, agrarian, and technical studies that would have been essential to make modernization work. No agrarian reforms corrected the misuse of the land. Modernization was pursued without eradicating labor abuses. (The abolition of slavery seemed to be as much a convenience for the landowners as a humanitarian act, and the slaves often were integrated into other old and iniquitous labor practices.) Although tariffs rose, they did not rise fast enough to provide the protection or encouragement extensive industrialization required. Industrialization of certain agrarian sectors—sugar is an excellent example—permitted the elites to continue to compete on the world market but did nothing to improve the quality of life of the masses. In fact, such agrarian modernization, as well as increasing land monopoly, often augmented the ranks of the unemployed, accelerating the flow of the jobless from the countryside into the cities, which were ill-prepared to absorb them. The export-oriented economy must bear a heavy share of the responsibility for filling the cities with rural folk unprepared to contribute to urban life and the consequent growth of slums and shantytowns, crime and delinquency, alcoholism and prostitution, a further marginalization of the folk. Taxes on the elites remained minimal and were easily avoided, depriving the governments of finances to carry out fundamental programs of modernization. Foreign interests received preference over national and belied any claims of the elite to nationalism. Since the elites had access to political power, they must bear the responsibilities for decisions made, the type of modernization imposed, and the failures of their programs to decrease dependency and to initiate development. Since the emerging middle class was coopted, identifying its goals more with the upper-class life-styles than with meaningful reform of old institutions, it too will have to bear a part of the responsibility.

The effects of cosmetic modernization satisfied the elites and seemed acceptable to the middle class, just as the consequences of thoroughly implementing the goal of real modernization frightened them. It is understandable: they profited from their relationship with the metropolis. In fact, they enjoyed the best of two worlds: the superficial modernization enhanced their immediate comforts and flattered their image of themselves, while at the same time permitting them to blame the "barbaric" masses for delaying or frustrating further modernization. By changing the social context—destroying folk societies, weakening folk culture, and substituting Western concepts of progress—the elites were able to dismay their numerous opponents, to reduce them to ineffectiveness, to ensure the continued and successful deterioration of the way of life they espoused.

The erosion of folk values and the stagnant or declining quality of life for the majority of the Latin Americans—particularly noticeable during the final quarter of the century—spoke to the broader tragedy of the elite's decisions on what constituted progress and the consequent failure to initiate development. While it is true that studies of the life-styles of ordinary people during the nineteenth century are scarce and that the research on the standards of living of the masses is only beginning to appear, it still seems warranted and necessary to posit these tentative conclusions for present discussion and future debate.

Access to land had been fundamental to defining the life-style of the rural masses. During the nineteenth century, the land that had supported the local populations of Latin America became increasingly commercialized to support bureaucrats, merchants, and absentee landlords. Everywhere the Indian communities were divested of whatever lands they still held at the time of independence. As a first step the liberal governments, beginning with that of Simón Bolívar, decreed the division of community lands into individual holdings, an imitation of capitalist patterns of Western Europe. The local latifundistas then found it easy to absorb the small, individual plots, although the landowners were not without myriad other resources to aggrandize their holdings. The outcome was the loss of land for the majority. Mexico perhaps represented an extreme: between 1876 and 1910 over 96 percent of the communal villages lost their lands. Former peasants became a type of landless, rural proletariat forced by a variety of measures, not least of which was hunger, to work the large estates. That new labor status accelerated their deculturation.

With one hand the governments facilitated the seizure of Indian and mestizo peasant lands, while with the other they conferred land titles on Europeans. The foreigners always found the governments more receptive to their land requirements than the natives did. In the last half of the century, the Argentine government routinely made land and financial aid available to immigrants which it denied to Argentines. After 1870 in Paraguay, land once available to everyone fell to the domain of the large landowners, many of whom were foreigners. The process was duplicated throughout Latin America, where the elites succeeded in imposing policies permitting them to acquire and/or expand estates, to deprive the peasants of their lands to ensure a labor force, and to pay low wages by maintaining a large (and landless) labor pool.

The latifundistas proved to be grossly inefficient users of the lands they monopolized. Evidence indicates that in many cases the utilization of the land decreased as the latifundium grew. The small rural plots produced more per unit of input, as well as provided more employment, than the typical large estate did. An increasingly large amount of the land that was put to the plow produced crops for export. In Panama in 1906, less than one percent of the country's land was cultivated, but fully one-third of the cultivated acres belonged to the United Fruit Company, which produced crops for export. Although an exporter of beef and wheat, Argentina found it necessary to import between 16 and 28 percent of its food supply during the years 1876–1896. Records in Mexico indicate that per capita production of the basic corn crop declined from 282 kilograms in 1877 to 154 in 1894 to 144 in 1907; yet Mexican export tonnage spiraled upward. The rural masses lost control over the land, their food supply, and ultimately their fate.

With diminishing access to land and as a result of commercialized agriculture, the rural masses suffered from declining real wages and standards of nutrition. Inflation in nineteenth-century Latin America drove prices upward; the prices rose faster than wages. The quality of life of the majority consequently deteriorated. Some recent research has focused on this theme, and it is appropriate at this time to review the literature.

Perhaps the most thorough documentation of the declining quality of life exists for rural Mexico. Seemingly the decline set in shortly after independence, although it must be emphasized that those declines affected the masses rather than the elites. A well-documented study such as that by Charles H. Harris III on the latifundio of the Sánchez Navarro family reveals that that family moved from the colonial into the national period without any losses. Due to careful management and political savvy the clan expanded its landholdings by the 1840s to over 25,000 square miles. The author also noted that while the Sánchez Navarros improved their already privileged position, the conditions for their peons deteriorated. With convincing statistics, scholars document that health, nutrition, and consumption levels for the Mexican rural laborers and their families fell over the course of the nineteenth century but most particularly during the Porfiriato. In 1810, total corn production averaged two pounds per Mexican per day; by 1919 it had fallen to less than one pound. It has been estimated that real wages in 1910 were but one-quarter of those of 1810. Contemporaneous commentators on the life-style of the rural Indian masses often observed that it was worse than during the colonial period. In 1834, *La Palabra* noted, "The Indians today find themselves in a worse situation than under the vice-royalty," an observation repeated in 1887 by *El Libre y Aceptado Masón:* "For them [the Indians], we are worse than the conquerors. The Indians are the docile instruments of the reactionaries, and if they look to the past it is because their present situation is worse than the old one." Alberto Santa Fé, founder of the periodical *La Revolución Social* and a federal deputy during the Porfiriato, observed:

> It is painful to say it, but it is true: they [the Indians] were happier, relatively, under the Spanish domination than they are under the protection of their own liberal and democratic government as we characterize ours. Yesterday they bore the title of slaves and were free. Today they are designated freemen but are slaves.

The misery of Mexico's Indian and mestizo masses increased to dismal proportions during the three and one half decades of the Díaz government. The buying power of rural wages slipped sharply during those years. In the Federal District, the price of corn tripled between 1887 and 1908, while that of beans nearly quadrupled between 1899 and 1908. The rural laborers were eating less of the basic agricultural crops in 1910 than they had in 1877.

The continuity in Argentine, Guatemalan, and Paraguayan history was less marked than in Mexico since in each of those three countries populist caudillos alternated in power with the Europeanized elites, permitting a contrast and comparison between the effects of the folk and Westernized governments on the quality of life of the masses. For all three nations, evidence seems to suggest that the rural poor enjoyed a better quality of life under the populist caudillos than under the rule of the Europeanized elites. In the case of Argentina, the gauchos enjoyed an access to land, freedom of movement, greater economic alternatives, and better living conditions during the Rosas period than at any time afterward. In contrast, during the last half, particularly the last quarter, of the century, their quality of life declined. The export boom benefited the large landowner but bypassed entire regions and whole social classes. Real wages of rural workers declined. Carl Solberg concluded that between 1884 and 1899, real wages fell a full 20 percent. In the province of Tucumán, the newspaper *La Razón* pointed out on several occasions in the 1880s that Brazilian slaves lived better than the local peons did. The sugar boom of that province in no way alleviated the misery and debt peonage, which became increasingly characteristic of the working class. For Guatemala, David M. McCreery has indicated the negative effects of coffee exports and national legislation on the Indians' standard of living during the last quarter of the century. The revisionists of Paraguayan history likewise emphasize the disaster of imported capitalism after 1870 on the life-styles of the masses. As this essay already has suggested, the increasing plight of the Guatemalan and Paraguayan peasants reversed the favorable situation they enjoyed under Carrera in the Central American republic and under Francia and the two Lópezes in the South American nation.

In a seminal study of Chilean rural labor, Arnold J. Bauer noted that rising export demands made on the haciendas after midcentury caused deterioration of the quality of life among the workers. The old stystem of *inquilinaje* became more demanding, imposing a heavier work load on rural labor while at the same time the *inquilinos* received smaller land allotments. By the last decade of the century, real wages "most likely" were falling. In another recent study of Chile, Brian Loveman concluded, "After 1860 wages in the countryside fell further and further behind the rising cost of food and basic necessities. The conditions of the inquilinos worsened as landlords required the service tenants to work more days, provide more family labor, or pay additional peons to fulfill the family's labor obligations." For Brazil, the coffee boom of the last half of the century brought prosperity to a limited region of the vast subcontinent. There per capita income increased, but those figures can be misleading. Nathaniel H. Leff warns us, "While the income of domestic landowners was increasing, the elastic supply of labor had a dampening effect on upward wage movements. Under these conditions, the growth in incomes

consequent upon export expansion probably led to an increase
in the inequality of income distribution within the expanding
export region." Whatever prosperity characterized the
Southeast had to be weighed with declines elsewhere in the
economy, particularly in the Northeast where the dominant
sugar industry was undergoing a series of prolonged crises. In
that region, real wages deteriorated after 1870 and the rural
wage earner suffered a falling standard of living. After an ex-
haustive study of that sugar industry, Peter L. Eisenberg concluded that "the free rural laborers in the later nineteenth
century enjoyed little material advantages over the slave." William Paul McGreevey in his *An Economic History of Colombia,
1845–1930* offers one of the most damning indictments of the
effects of the pseudo-European institutions on the welfare of
the majority. McGreevey concluded, "Income apparently declined for significant groups of the Colombian population in
the second half of the nineteenth century." The purchasing
power of the rural wage earner of the basic foods: corn, meat,
flour, and potatoes, fell approximately 50 percent between
1848 and 1892. From the evidence now at hand, a preliminary
conclusion can be drawn that deprived of land, offered low
salaries whose buying power diminished over the course of a
century, and forced to subsist on an increasingly restricted and
less nutritious diet, the rural masses suffered from a declining
quality of life as the century waned.

The above discussion concentrated on the rural sector because an overwhelming majority of the Latin Americans in the
nineteenth century lived in the countryside and because more
data on their standard of living is available. Probably the situation for the majority of the urban dwellers was no better.
McGreevey disclosed a shift of income in urban Colombia away
from poor artisans to well-to-do merchants. Real industrial
wages in Mexico amounted to less in 1910 than they had been a
generation earlier. Those wages barely met the minimum needs
of the workers, who by 1900 were spending as much as 60
percent of their earnings on food. At that, the diet probably
was insufficient and the workers underfed. Industrialization
brought no boon to the Mexican working class.

James R. Scobie provided some valuable, if bleak statistics
on the rising cost of living in Buenos Aires, 1870–1910. Although alternating with some periods of recovery, the wages for

day laborers in the Argentine capital slid from 1.20 gold pesos in 1871 to .50 in 1897 but rose to .55 by 1901 and recovered to the 1871 level by 1910. Skilled construction workers earned a daily wage of 4.00 gold pesos in 1871, which fell to .85-1.00 in 1897 and then recovered but by 1910 was still 2.10-2.70 gold pesos, considerably below the 1871 figure. While wages declined over the period the cost of living rose. A small room in a crowded *conventillo* rented fro 4-8 gold pesos a month in 1871; 8-10 by 1890; and 12-14 by 1911. Understandably during that period of declining wages and rising rents, the number of inhabitants per room increased. Scobie concluded that the cost of living for the urban working class was disporportionately high. He left us with this economic conundrum: "The top monthly wage a day laborer could earn [in 1901] amounted to 70 pesos *moneda nacional* (m$n), or the equivalent of 30 gold pesos. The estimated minimum expenses for an average worker family totaled 100 pesos m$n, or 43 gold pieces."

Aldo Ferrer also testified that prices outstripped wages in the Argentine cities, allocating to the workers a small share of the income generated by industry; and in her studies of wages and prices in Rio de Janeiro, Eulalia M. L. Lobo noted, "A general tendency of lower acquisitive power of salaries manifested itself in the second half of the nineteenth century." Increasingly other research in other areas of Latin America reveals the same urban pattern.

The ultimate conclusion for some of the impoverished masses at least was early death through malnutrition, hunger, and lack of adequate medical care. In the words of the Mexican intellectual Francisco Bulnes, the fall of real wages resulted in the inevitable "death by hunger." The statistical evidence is still not at hand to document this conclusion properly. But perhaps these figures from Venezuela on the deaths per one thousand inhabitants suggest the propensity to that conclusion:

1840 - 20.4
1850 - 18.2
1875 - 21.9
1885 - 24.5
1895 - 21.1
1905 - 21.7

Recent studies of Recife, a major Brazilian city, at the turn of the century, also reveal a rising death rate of somewhat more dramatic dimensions. The city's death rate had averaged about 32–34 per thousand for much of the nineteenth century, but by 1895 it rose to 40 where it remained for nearly a decade. Eduardo E. Arriago offers more optimistic figures of a different nature. Of the five countries (Brazil, Costa Rica, Guatemala, Mexico, and Paraguay) for which he provides some nineteenth-century data on the expectation of life at birth, all showed a rising life expectancy. However, his statistics and the conclusions derived from them have been challenged. While figures for nineteenth-century Latin America are suspect, a life expectancy of 28.9 years has been suggested for 1910. A rise in the death rate in Venezuela and in Recife as well as the low life expectance for Latin America in general occurred during a century notable for its rapid and phenomenal medical advances, and beg explanation.

For the majority, the heritage of modernization was proving to be increased concentration of land in the hands of ever fewer owners, falling per capita food production with the corollary rising food imports, greater improvement, less to eat, more vulnerability to the whims of an impersonal international market, uneven growth, increased unemployment and under-employment, social, economic, and political marginalization, and greater power in the hands of the privileged few. To the degree the folk cultures and societies were forced to integrate into world commerce, the fewer the benefits the folk would reap. But poverty through progress in nineteenth-century Latin America must be understood in more than material terms and declining wages, purchasing power, or nutritional levels. A tragic spiritual and cultural impoverishment debased those folk forced by circumstances to give up previously satisfactory ways of life and to accept alien ones that provided them little or no psychic benefits. They were cut adrift from their own past and unable or unwilling to adjust to the Westernization that came to dominate the bureaucratic apparatus increasingly shaping their lives.

Extremes in opulence and simplicity, comfort and deprivation in life-styles always had characterized Latin America, whether we talk of the Indian empires, the viceregal system, or the independence period. But one of the most notable characteristics of the nineteenth century was the widening of that gap into a chasm. Economic growth, confined to a narrow economic sector involved in export, aggravated the inequities of income and the differences in the qualities of life. An increasing rate of economic growth in that select sector further unbalanced income distribution by concentrating the wealth in fewer hands. The industrialization accompanying selective modernization likewise favored the wealthy at the expense of the poor. In short, under the institutional structures characteristics of nineteenth-century Latin America, the poor majority faced a bleak and deteriorating position whether or not economic growth occurred. However, the elites' urge to export and to modernize exacerbated the position of the majority. So, while the quality of life of the majority deteriorated, the lifestyle of the elites and to a lesser extent of the emerging middle class improved, both to extremes previously unequaled. But more than economic extremes separated the elites from the masses. As the elites became more Europeanized, the cultural distance between them and the vast majority of their fellow citizens also widened. The elites became strangers in their own nations and lost their environmental perspective.

The poor both bore the burden of the inequitable institutional structures and paid for the modernization enjoyed by the privileged. In practice, the progress pursued by the elites further impoverished the masses. The deprivation, repression, and deculturation of the majority by the minority over the course of decades created tensions that frequently gave rise to violence. The poor protested their accelerating misfortunes as modernization increased. For their own part, the privileged were determined to modernize and to maintain the order required to do so. They freely used whatever force was necessary to accomplish both. Consequently, the imposition of unmediated modernization brough more social disorder than progress.

The majority in the long run was uniformly unsuccessful in implementing its desires. In part, they lacked the armaments and trained armies at the disposal of the elites who, when the going got particularly rough, could rely on outside support in the form of loans, arms shipments, and armed intervention. Brazil did not hesitate in 1852 to invade Argentina and with Argentine allies to overthrow Juan Manuel de Rosas. Brazil and Argentina, relying on English loans, arms, and advice, fought

Paraguay, annihilated its army, and destroyed its socioeco-
nomic-political systems during the War of the Triple Alliance.
British attitudes toward the Cruzob were fundamental to the
Mayas' early successes and ultimate defeat, when arms first sold
to the Cruzob through British Honduras were later withheld.
Principally, however, the majority failed for lack of coordinated effort. Putting aside the exceptional cases of Argentina,
Paraguay, Bolivia, Guatemala, and Yucatan, the widespread
violence in Latin America was generally individual cases of
protest against specific injustices. Cumulatively it was impressive, but with the exceptions noted, it lacked a focal point, a
coordinated drive, a central leadership. It was a violence
engaged in by the folk, to some extent by the rural patriarchs,
but hardly at all by the dissident intellectuals. The diffusion
gave the elites a tremendous advantage. They could deal with
each individual incidence of violence separately and crush it
with their armies. They did.

Hypothetically the alternatives to the progress through
modernization as imposed by the nineteenth-century elites were
at least two. First, through greater mediation of novelties, the
folk societies might have admitted change more slowly, selectively, and salutarily. Such an alternative struck a middle
course, eschewing a return to the past or a rejection of further
modernization as well as the unquestioned acceptance of everything foreign and new. There was at least one example of its
temporary success: Paraguay under the folk caudillos seems to
be the nation in nineteenth-century Latin America that offers
the best example of genuine development as contrasted with
growth. Further, some modernization accompanied that development. True, the life-style of the rustic Paraguayan population was simple in the extreme. Yet, if recent research is
correct, the people had access to land, ate a nourishing diet,
enjoyed adequate housing and minimal education, identified
with their caudillos, and felt the satisfaction of close communal
life. In short, the quality of life for the majority was satisfactory
or better. There is reason to believe that nowhere else in Latin
America over such a long time span did the majority so benefit.

The second alternative was total change, the restructuring
of all inherited institutions to the benefit of the majority. This
alternative would have required a revolution of far-reaching

magnitude, whose first victims would have been the land and labor systems inherited from the colonial period and strengthened during the nineteenth century. It would have recognized the cooperative, not the competitive, characteristics of the majority, their inclination toward communal living, rather than toward individualism. At least one intellectual of the early twentieth century, Peru's José Carlos Mariátegui, proposed the arresting idea that such a revolution was a return to the essence of the Indian past. To his thinking, Incan tradition inculcated socialism, and the modern socialism he advocated sprang from that Indian experience. The barrier separating that tradition from a new experiment with socialism was the complex of Spanish institutions imposed on Peru, most notably the latifundia. Spain forcibly had interrupted Peru's natural socialist evolution. Mariátegui wrote, "The true revolutionaries never proceed as if history will begin with them. They know that they represent an historic force. . . . There is no conflict between the revolutionary and tradition, for the revolutionary is in tune with history." Thus, in Mariátegui's eyes, the establishment of socialism in twentieth-century Peru fits well into the patterns of the past, linking the Incas with the present. Although perhaps some suggestions of revolutionary change were present in the early independence movements of Haiti and Mexico, Latin America would have to wait until the twentieth century before any experiment with such total change would take place.

Both of these alternatives recognize the contributions of the folk societies. Indeed, the well-being of the majority of the Latin Americans could not be served without including their preferences, their influence, and their contributions. To exclude their contributions has been to marginalize them.

Broadening the view of Latin America's recent past to include the intense cultural conflicts between the elites and the folk opens a wide range of infrequently mentioned topics, not the least of which would be a discussion of communal life-styles advocated by the majority. It brings modernization and the elites' faith in it into sharper focus. Such a view diversifies an otherwise homogeneous history as well as focusing attention on the plurality of solutions to Latin America's problems of development. It offers an interpretation that gives greater meaning to the diverse events in nineteenth-century Latin America. It was not, after all, a century of random conflicts, meaningless civil wars, and pervasive chaos, but one in which those who favored modernization struggled with those loyal to their folk societies and cultures. Finally, it provides one insight into the constant and major enigma of Latin America: prevalent poverty in a potentially wealthy region. The triumph of progress as defined by the elites set the course for twentieth-century history. It bequeathed a legacy of mass poverty and continued conflict.

CHAPTER NOTES

Chapter 2

p. 20. The ideas of José Avelino Aramayo are discussed in Carlos Medinaceli, *La Inactualidad de Alcides Argüedas e Otros Estudios Biográficos* (La Paz: Los Amigos del Libro, 1972), pp. 93-94.

p. 20. The Prado quote comes from Thomas E. Skidmore, "Eduardo Prado: A Conservative Nationalist Critic of the Early Brazilian Republic, 1889-1901," *Luso-Brazilian Review* 12, 2 (Winter 1975: 149.

pp. 21-22. For the Echeverría statement consult José Luis Romero, *A History of Argentine Political Thought* (Stanford, Calif.: Stanford University Press, 1963), p. 145. Similar ideas pervaded the constitutions of some southern states of the United States at the end of the nineteenth century. Under the Hawaiian Republic declared in 1893 principally by U.S. sugar planters and merchants on the islands, the vote was reserved for the propertied few. In 1900 Sanford Dole, governor designate of the Territory of Hawaii, opined that native Hawaiians should not be allowed to vote "simply because they were grown up. I believe it is exceedingly necessary to keep out of politics this class of people, irresponsible people I mean. . . . " Quoted by Gavan Daws, *Shoal of Time: A History of the Hawaiian Islands* (Honolulu: The University Press of Hawaii, 1974), p. 294.

p. 22. Félix Avelino Aramyo's ideas are found in Medinaceli, *La Inactualidad*, p. 144.

pp. 22-23. D. F. Sarmiento, *Life in the Argentine Republic in the Days of the Tyrants; Or, Civilization and Barbarism* (New York: Hafner, n.d.), p. 42.

pp. 23-24. The fears of President Mascarenhas will be found in *Relatório que à Assemblea Legislativa de Goyaz Apresentou na Sessão Ordinária de 1845 o Exm. Presidente de Mesma Província D. José de Assiz Mascarenhas* (Goyaz, Brazil: Typ. Provincial, 1845), p. 13. The fears of Governor Vallarta were quoted in Jean Meyer, *Problemas Campesinos y Revueltas Agrarias (1821-1910)* (Mexico City: Sep-Setentas, 1973), p. 115.

pp. 26-27. Clorinda Matto de Turner, *Aves Sin Nido* (Buenos Aires: Solar/Hachette, 1968), pp. 38; ibid., 15-16, 19, 167.

pp. 28-29. Enclydes da Cunha, *Rebellion in the Backlands* (Chicago: University of Chicago Press, 1957), pp. 464, 78, 481, 408, 54.

p. 30. Jorge Moreal, "Americanismo," *Dom Quixote* (Rio de Janeiro) 1, 8 (1895): 3.

pp. 30–31. Much of the information on Mexico comes from T. G. Powell, "Mexican Intellectuals and the Indian Question, 1876–1911," *Hispanic American Historical Review* 48, 1 (February 1968): 37-58.

pp. 31–32. Information on the Central American intellectuals' attitudes towards the Indians comes from Darío González, *Primer Congreso Pedagógico Centroamericano* (1893) (Guatemala City: Tip. Nacional, 1894); Jesús Julian Amurrio González, *El Positivismo en Guatemala* (Guatemala City: Editorial Universitaria, 1970), pp. 97–101.

p. 32. General Roca's Order of the Day will be found in Mark S. W. Jefferson, *Peopling the Argentine Pampas* (New York: American Geographical Society, 1926), pp. 90-91.

Chapter 3

p. 35. The sixty-three historians upon whose life and work the information contained in this chapter is based are:

João Capistrano de Abreu (1853-1927), Brazil;
Cecilio Acosta (1818-1881), Venezuela;
Lucas Alamán (1792-1853), Mexico;
Juan Bautista Alberdi (1810-1884), Argentina;
Miguel Luis Amunátegui (1828-1888), Chile;
Pedro de Angelis (1784-1859), Argentina;
Mariano Arosemena (1794-1868), Department of Panamá, Colombia;
Diego Barros Arana (1830-1907), Chile;
Januário da Cunha Barbosa (1780-1846), Brazil;
Francisco Bauzá (1849-1899), Uruguay;
Eduardo Blanco (1838-1912), Venezuela;
Carlos María de Bustamante (1774-1848), Mexico;
Pedro Fermín Cevallos (1812-1893), Ecuador;
Luis L. Dominguez (1819-1898), Argentina;
José Esteban Echeverría (1805-1851), Argentina;
José Manuel Estrada (1842-1897), Argentina;
Joaquín García Icazbalceta (1825-1894), Mexico;
Juana Manuela Gorriti (1819-1892), Argentina;
José Manuel Groot (1800-1878), Colombia;
Paul Groussac (1848-1929), Argentina;
José Inácio de Abreu e Lima (1794-1869), Brazil;
João Francisco Lisboa (1812-1863), Brazil;
Lucio Vicente López (1848-1894), Argentina;
Vicente Fidel López (1815-1903), Argentina;
Sebastián Lorente (1813-1884), Peru;
Agostinho Marques Perdigão Malheiro (1828-1881), Brazil;
Alejandro Marure (1809-1851), Guatemala;
José Toribio Medina (1852-1930), Chile;
Francisco Inácio Marcondes Homem de Melo (1837-1918), Brazil;

Manuel de Mendiburu (1805-1885), Peru;
José Milla y Viduarre (1822-1882), Guatemala;
Bartolomé Mitre (1821-1906), Argentina;
Pedro Moncayo (1804-1888), Ecuador;
Lorenzo Montúfar y Rivera Maestre (1823-1898), Guatemala;
José María Luis Mora (1794-1850), Mexico;
Alesandre José de Melo Morais (1816-1882), Brazil;
Gabriel René Moreno (1834-1908), Bolivia;
Joaquim Nabuco (1849-1910), Brazil;
Manuel de Odriozola (1804-1889), Peru;
Manuel Orozco y Berra (1816-1881), Mexico;
José Maria da Silva Paranhos, Júnior, Baron of Rio-Branco (1845-1912), Brazil;
Mariano Filipe Paz Soldán (1821-1886), Peru;
Pedro Paz Soldán y Unánue (1839-1895), Peru;
Antonio Pereira Pinto (1819-1880), Brazil;
Ernesto Quesada (1858-1934), Argentina;
Carlos María Ramírez (1848-1898), Uruguay;
José Manuel Restrepo (1781-1863), Colombia;
Ernesto Restrepo Tirado (1862-1896), Colombia;
Vicente Riva Palacio (1832-1896), Mexico
Sílvio Romero (1851-1914), Brazil;
Adolfo Saldía (1850-1914), Argentina;
Domingo Faustino Sarmiento (1811-1888), Argentina;
Justo Sierra Méndez (1848-1912), Mexico;
Inácio Accioli de Cerqueira de Silva (1808-1865), Brazil;
Joaquim Caetano da Silva (1810-1873), Brazil;
Joaquim Norberto de Sousa Silva (1820-1891), Brazil;
Ramón Sotomayor y Valdés (1830-1903), Chile;
Alfredo D'Escragnolle Taunay (1843-1889), Brazil;
Manuel Ricardo Trelles (1821-1893), Argentina;
Francisco Adolfo de Varnhagen (1816-1878), Brazil;
Dalmacio Vélez Sarsfield (1800-1875), Argentina;
Benjamín Vicuña Mackenna (1831-1886), Chile;
Antonio Zinny (1821-1890), Argentina.

p. 36. Andrés Bello, "Modo de Escribir la Historia," *El Araucano* (Santiago, 1845), republished in *Obras Completas* (Santiago: Ramírez, 1884), VII, 116-117.

p. 37. Rafael Montúfar, *La Historia: Conferencia Dada en el Salón de Actos de la Facultad de Derecho y Notariado del Central El 1º de Mayo de 1900* (Guatemala City: Tip. Sánchez & de Guise, 1900).

p. 37. Francisco Bilbao, *Obras Completas de Francisco Bilbao* (Santiago: Imprenta de Buenos Aires, 1865), I, 17.

p. 39. Blanco Fombona was quoted in Jean Franco, *The Modern Culture of Latin America: Society and the Artist* (New York: Praeger, 1967), p. 42.

p. 40. Vicente Fidel López is quoted in Rómulo D. Carbia, *His-*

toria de la Historiografía Argentina (La Plata: Biblioteca Humanidades, 1925), p. 54, n. 3. Januário da Cunha Barbosa, "Iconographía Brazileira," *Revista do Instituto Histórico e Geográfico Brasileiro* 19 (1856): 353.

p. 41. The quotation from Diego Barros Arana will be found in Francisco A. Encina, *La Literatura Histórica Chilena y el Concepto Actual de la Historia* (Santiago: Editorial Nascimento, 1935), p. 63.

p. 41. Januário da Cunha Barbosa, "Discursos," *Revista do Instituto Histórico e Geográfico Brasileiro* 1 (1839): 17-18.

p. 41. The quotation from Vicente Fidel López comes from Allen L. Wall, "The Philosophy of History in Nineteenth-Century Chile: The Lastarria-Bello Debates," *History and Theory* 13, 3 (Fall 1974): 276.

p. 43. Juan Antonio Oddone, "La Historiografía Uruguaya en el Siglo XIX: Apuntes para su Estudio," *Revista Histórica de la Universidad, Segunda Epoca, 1 (Montevideo, February 1959): 3. Federico González Suárez, Defensa de mi Criterio Histórico* (Quito, 1937), p. 80.

pp. 45-46. Vicente Fidel López was quoted in Alberto Pla, *Ideología y Método en la Historiografía Argentina* (Buenos Aires: Ediciones Nueva Visión, 1972), p. 29. For the statement of Mitre see Museo Mitre, *Correspondencia Literaria, Histórica y Política del General Bartolomé* (Buenos Aires: Coni Hermanos, 1912), III, 284.

p. 46. The Diego Barros Arana quotes come from Encina, *La Literatura Histórica Chilena*, p. 44.

p. 46. Mariano Zecena, *La Reforma: Revolución de 1871 y sus Caudillos*, 3d ed. (Guatemala City: Ministerio de Educación Pública, 1957), p. 64. The first edition appeared in 1898.

p. 47. Mitre's statement can be found in Museo Mitre, *Correspondencia*, III, 284.

Chapter 4

p. 53. Alberdi's change of opinion towards Rosas is documented in Nicanor Eduardo Colombres, "Alberdi y Rosas," *Revisión Histórica* 2 (Tucumán, May 1961), pp. 77-82. Alberdi's denunciation of *Civilazación y Barbarie* is discussed in Fermin Chávez, *Civilización y Barbarie en la Historia de Cultura Argentina* (Buenos Aires: Ediciones Theoría, 1974), p. 56. For the quotations from Alberdi see Juan Bautista Alberdi, *Obras Completas* (Buenos Aires: Imprenta de la Tribuna Nacional, 1887), IV, 69; VII, 156; *Escritos Postumos* (Buenos Aires: Imprenta Europa, 1898), X, 241.

p. 53. José Maria Dalence, *Bosquejo Estadístico de Bolivia* (Chuquisaca: Imprenta de Sucre, 1851), pp. 220-221. For information on the "Representación" see Juan Bustamante, *Los Indios del Perú* (Lima: Monterola, 1867), p. 22. *El Nacional* (Lima), 17 May 1867. The two short stories by Daniel Mendoza can be read in the 1922 edition of *El Llanero* (Caracas: Tip. Cultura Venezolana, 1922).

p. 54. The information on and quotes from Alberdi will be found in *Obras Completas*, IV, 68: VII, 166; VIII, 164-165. His concept of progress is discussed in José Ingenieros, *La Evolución de las Ideas Argentinas* (Buenos Aires: El Ateno, 1951), II, 499.

p. 55. Adam Ferguson, *An Essay on the History of Civil Society* (Edinburgh: University of Edinburgh Press, 1966), pp. 105-106. José Joaquín Fernández de Lizardi, *El Periquillo Sarnieto* (Mexico: Porrua, 1963), p. 319.

pp. 55-56. Sebastião Ferreira Soares, *Notas Estatísticas sôbre a Produção Agrícola e Carestia dos Generos Alimentícios no Império do Brasil*, 2d. ed. (Rio de Janeiro: IPEA/INPES, 1977), pp. 78-80. The first edition bears the date 1860.

p. 56. The ideas of José Martí on progress are found in *Páginas Escogidas* (Havana: Editora Universitaria, 1965), Vol. 1, 385. His thoughts on the rural masses can be consulted in his *Obras Completas* (Havana: Editora Nacional, 1965), Vol. 8, 290.

p. 57. The quotations from Col. Alvaro Gabriel Barros, *Actualidad Financiera de la República Argentina* (Buenos Aires: Imp. Librarias de Mayo, 1875), as reprinted in *La Opinión Cultural* (Buenos Aires), 7 June 1975.

p. 58. Ramón Ramírez, *El Cristianismo y la Libertad: Ensayo sobre la Civilización Americana* (Caracas: Imprenta de V. Espinal, 1885), p. XII. Germán Carrera Damas has made an excellent summary and analysis of this book in his *Temas de Historia Social y de las Ideas* (Caracas: Ediciones de la Biblioteca de la Universidad Central de Venezuela, 1969), pp. 139-165.

pp. 58-59. Tulio Febres Cordero, *Don Quijote en America: O Sea la Cuarta Salida del Ingenioso Hidalgo de la Mancha* included in his *Obras Completas* (Bogotá: Antares, 1960), V, 48, 89-90.

pp. 60-61. José Hernández, *The Gaucho Martín Fierro* (Albany: State University of New York Press, 1974), pp. 84-85, 83.

pp. 62-63. Sílvio Romero, *História da Literatura Brasileira*, 2d ed. (Rio de Janeiro: H. Garnier, 1902), 1, 11, 102.

p. 64. The quote from José de Alencar appeared in Norman Winkler, "The *Sertão* in the *Romances* of Four Brazilian Writers" (Ph.D. diss., Department of Modern Language and Literature, University of Pittsburgh, 1960), p. 90.

p. 64. The poem of Juan E. O'Leary appeared in José Rodríguez Alcalá, ed., *Antología Paraguaya* (Asunción, 1911).

p. 65. Bustamante, *Los Indios del Perú*, p. 95.

p. 66. *Diario de Pernambuco* (Recife), 24 March 1856.

p. 66. Ferreira Soares, *Notas Estatísticas*, pp. 279–280, 19–20, 133–134.

p. 67. The quotation from Francisco Severo Maldonado will be found in Meyer, *Problemas Campesinos*, pp. 36–37.

p. 68. In 1904, Manuel González Prada wrote that the Indian question is not one of education but of economics. *Horas de Luchas* (Lima: Persa, 1969). That idea is the subject of his essay "Nuestros Indios." The Mariátegui quote comes from *Seven Interpretive Essays on Peruvian Reality* (Austin: University of Texas Press, 1974), p. 22.

p. 70. João Capistrano de Abreu, "O Caracter Nacional e as Origens do Povo Brasileiro," *O Globo* (Rio de Janeiro), 9 March 1876.

p. 70. João Capistrano de Abreu, *Ensaios e Estudos* (Rio de Janeiro: Briguiet, 1931), I, iii.

Chapter 5

p. 77. The statement by Rufino Cuevo is quoted in Jaime Jaramillo Uribe, *El Pensamiento Colombiano en el Siglo XIX* (Bogotá: Editorial Temis, 1964), p. 33.

p. 78. Cross presents his information on the standard of living of the workers on the Hacienda del Maguey in his essay, "Living Standards in Rural Nineteenth-Century Mexico: Zacatecas, 1820–80," *Journal of Latin American Studies* 10, 1 (May 1978): 1–19.

p. 79. The statement against equality was quoted in Gilberto Freyre, *The Mansions and the Shanties: The Making of Modern Brazil* (New York: Knopf, 1963), p. 242.

pp. 81–83. Ignacio Manuel Altamirano, *Christmas in the Mountains* (Gainesville: University of Florida Press, 1961), pp. 48–49, 6–7, 66, 57.

p. 83. Joaquín V. González, *Mis Montañas* (Buenos Aires: Editorial Kapelusy, 1965), p. xix.

pp. 84–85. Luis Orrego Luco, *Casa-Grande* (Santiago: Zig-Zag, 1961), pp. 55–56, 68.

Chapter 6

pp. 86–87. Romero, *A History of Argentine Political Thought*, pp. 82–89.

p. 87. Roberto Cortés Conde, *The First Stages of Modernization in Spanish America* (New York: Harper and Row, 1974), p. 117.

pp. 87–91. Although these paragraphs reflect some influence of Robert Redfield, "The Folk Society," *The American Journal of Sociology* 52, 4 (January 1947): 293–308; Gideon Sjoberg, "Folk and Feudal Societies," *The American Journal of Sociology* 58, 3 (November 1952): 231-239; I feel most indebted to the ideas of George M. Foster, "What is Folk Culture?" *American Anthropologist* 55, 2, pt. 1 (April-June, 1953): 159-173.

p. 91. Mariátegui's ideas on folk leadership are found in his *Seven Interpretative Essays,* p. 50.

pp. 91–92. The quotations from Alberdi will be found in Romero, *History of Argentine Political Thought,* pp. 124, 127; in Juan Bautista Alberdi, *Grandes y Pequeños Hombres del Plata,* 4th ed. (Buenos Aires: Editorial Plus Ultra, 1974), pp. 154, 161, 155.

p. 92. Manuel Gálvez, "Vida de Aparicio Saravia," in *Biografías Completas de Manuel Gálvez* (Buenos Aires: Emecé Editores, 1962).

p. 94. Rodolfo Ortega Peña and Eduardo Luis Duhalde suggest how popular songs of the 1860s can be used to revise the standard historical view of that period. *Folklore Argentino y Revisionismo Histórico* (Buenos Aires: Editorial Sudestada, 1967). Also see Leonardo Paso, *Los Caudillos: Historia o Folklore* (Buenos Aires: Silaba, 1969). On the Brazilian folk narrative, consult Emílio F. Moran, "Some Semantic Categories in Brazilian Caboclo Folk Narratives," *Luso-Brazilian Review* 11, 2 (Winter 1974): 221. The information about and quotation from the Mexican corrido are from Merle E. Simmons, *The Mexican Corrido as a Source for Interpretive Study of Modern Mexico (1870–1950)* (Bloomington: Indiana University Press, 1957), pp. 7, 33.

p. 95. The proverb is Ecuadorian and appears in Paulo de Carvalho-Neto, *El Folklore de las Luchas Sociales* (Mexico: Siglo Veintiuno Editores, 1973), p. 155.

p. 98. The revisionist analysis of the Carrera years in Guatemalan history is based largely on the following sources: Ralph Lee Woodward, Jr., *Social Revolution in Guatemala: The Carrera Revolt* (New Orleans; Tulane University, 1971); Keith L. Miceli, "Rafael Carrera: Defender and Promoter of Peasant Interests in Guatemala," *The Americas* 31, 1 (July 1974): 72-95; Max Leon Moorhead, "Rafael Carrera of Guatemala; His Life and Times," (Ph.D. diss., University of California, Berkeley, 1942); Manuel Coronado Aguilar, *El General Rafael Carrera ante la Historia* (Guatemala City: La Editorial del Ejército, 1965); Manuel Coronado Aguilar, *Apuntes Histórico-Guatemalenses* (Guatemala City: Editorial José de Pineda Ibarra, 1975); Clemente Marroquín Rojas, *Morazán y Carrera* (Guatemala City: Editorial José de Pineda Ibarra, 1971). The Carrera quotations come from Rafael Carrera, *Informe que Dirijó Presidente de la República de Guatemala al Cuerpo Representivo, en su Instalación el Día de Agosto de 1848* (Guatemala City: Imprenta de la Paz, 1848), pp. 2-3. *El Noticioso* (Guatemala City), 26 October 1861.

p. 98. Manuel Coronado Aguilar provides the quote on "a government of the people" in his *El General Rafael Carrera,* pp. 54–55. *El Tiempo* (Guatemala City), 30 August 1839.

p. 100. The Sacatepequez decree is in Sotero Carrera, *Bando de Policia y Buen Gobierno Expedido para el Departamento de Sacatepequez por su Corregidor y Comandante General Brigadier Sr. Sotero Carrera* (Guatemala City: Imprenta de la Aurora, 1849).

p. 100. The 1851 Carrera land decree is quoted in Coronado Aguilar, *Apuntes Histórico-Guatemalenses,* p. 486. On the issue of land and agrarian diversification see also pp. 482–483 and 485 of Coronado Aguilar as well as p. 37 of his *El General rafael Carrera;* Woodward, *Social Revolution in Guatemala,* p. 68; Moorhead, "Rafael Carrera," pp. 92, 190. Examples of the government's concern with communal lands can be found in the Archivo General de Centro América, Guatemala City, B100.1, Exp. 33282, Leg. 1419 dated 12 April 1841; B100.1, Exp. 33274, Leg. 1419 dated 29 November 1841; B100.0, Exp., 33305, Leg. 1419 dated 14 November 1843; B100.1, Exp. 33356, Leg. 1419 dated 2 November 1844; B100.1, Exp. 5307, Leg. 3633 dated 15 March 1853: and B100.1 Exp. 33326, Leg. 1419 dated 19 April 1863.

pp. 101–102. Carrera, *Informe,* pp. 3, 9–10. "El Antagonismo de Razas," *El Noticioso* (Guatemala City), 26 September 1862; Miguel Boada y Balmes, "Fantasia," *EL Noticioso,* 17 October 1862.

p. 102. Elisha Oscar Crosby, *Memoirs of Elisha Oscar Crosby: Reminiscenses of California and Guatemala from 1849 to 1864* (San Marino, Calif.: The Huntington Library, 1945), p. 97.

p. 103. Examples of newspaper comments on "progress" can be found in *El Noticioso,* 19 October and 11 December 1861; the editorial of *La Semana* (Guatemala City), 18 January 1865. Carrera's own remarks on barbarism and civilization are contained in his *Informe,* p. 12.

pp. 103–104. Felipe de Jesús, *María, Historia de una Mártir,* 2d ed. (Guatemala City: Editorial José de Pineda Ibarra, 1967), pp. 27–28, 29, 30, 175.

p. 105. For anthropological evidence of the shock of the coffee plantation on the Indians' culture see Oliver La Farge, "Maya Ethnology: The Sequence of Cultures," in *The Maya and Their Neighbors* (New York: Appleton-Century, 1962), p. 291; and Alfonso Villa Rojas, "The Concepts of Space and Time among the Contemporary Maya," in Miguel Leon Portilla, *Time and Reality in the Thought of the Maya* (Boston: Beacon Press, 1973), p. 117. José A. Beteta, *Edmundo* (Guatemala City: Tip. Nacional, 1896), pp. 23–24.

p. 106. Scant and contradictory data exist on Manuel Belzu. The interpretation in this essay is based largely on information from

Manuel José Cortés, *Ensayo sobre la Historia de Bolivia* (Sucre: Imprenta de Beeche, 1861); Enrique Finot, *Nueva Historia de Bolivia: Ensayo de Interpretación Sociológica,* 2d ed. (La Paz: Gisbert, 1954); Guillermo Lora, *Historia del Movimiento Obrero Boliviano, 1848–1900* (La Paz: Editorial Los Amigos del Libro, 1967); Fausto Reinaga, *Belzu: Precursor de la Revolución Nacional* (La Paz: Ediciones Rumbo Sindical, 1953); and José Fellmann Velarde, *Historia de Bolivia. La Bolivianidad Semifeudal,* Vol. 2 (La Paz: Editorial Los Amigos del Libro, 1970).

p. 106. M. León Favre-Clavairoz, *La Bolivie: Son Présent, Son Passé, Son Avenir* (Paris: Dubuisson, 1857).

p. 107. Information on the articles in *El Estandarte* comes from Guillermo Lora, *Historia del Movimiento Obrero Boliviano,* p. 94. Dalence, *Bosquejo Estadístico de Bolivia,* p. 308.

p. 108. The three quotations of Belzu come from José Fellmann Velarde, *Historia de Bolivia,* II, 119.

pp. 108–109. Belzu's remarks to and about the people of Cochabamba come from Manuel José Cortés, *Ensayo sobre la Historia de Bolivia,* pp. 202–203.

p. 109. The quotation from Belzu will be found in José Fellmann Velarde, *Historia de Bolivia,* II, 122.

p. 109. Of the two quotations from Belzu, the first comes from Guillermo Lora, *Historia del Movimiento Obrero Boliviano,* p. 352; the second from Enrique Finot, *Nueva Historia de Bolivia,* p. 238. The judgment on the 1855 elections is from José Fellmann Velarde, *Historia de Bolivia,* II, 135.

p. 112. The attitudes of the elite of Yucutan are from Nelson Reed, *The Caste War of Yucatan* (Stanford, Calif.: Stanford University Press, 1964), p. 61.

p. 113. Oswaldo Albornoz P., *Las Luchas Indígenas en el Ecuador* (Guayaquil: Editorial Claridad, nd), pp. 30–50.

p. 114. Benjamín Vicuña Mackenna, *Obras Completas de Vicuña Mackenna* (Santiago: Editorial Universidad de Chile, 1939), XII, 400; XIII, 432.

p. 114. Cirilo Villaverde, *Cecilia Valdes o La Loma del Angel* (Havana: Instituto Cubano del Libro, 1972), II, 184.

p. 115. The quotation from the president of Bahia comes from João José Reis, "A Elite Baiana Face os Movimentos Socialas, Bahia: 1824–1840," *Revista de História* (São Paulo), vol. 54, no. 108, ano 27 (1976), p. 382. Alberto Silva, "A Tragédia de Lucas da Feira," in *Tres Estudos de História* (Salvador: Progresso, 1955), p. 59.

p. 116. Prince Adalbert, *Travels in the South of Europe and in Brazil* (London, 1849), II, 43–44. William D. Piersen, "Puttin' Down

Ole Massa: African Satire in the New World," in Daniel J. Crowley, *African Folklore in the New World* (Austin: University of Texas Press, 1977), p. 31.

p. 118. On Vicente Ferreira da Paula, see Manuel Correia de Andrade, "The Social and Ethnic Significance of the War of the Cabanos," in Ronald H. Chilcote, ed., *Protest and Resistance in Angola & Brazil: Comparative Studies* (Berkeley, Los Angeles, London: University of California Press, 1972), p. 103. Hélio Vianna, *História do Brasil* (São Paulo: Edições Melhoramentos, 1961), II, 118.

p. 119. Information on and quotations from the Quebra-Quilo Revolt come from Roderick J. Barman, "The Brazilian Peasantry Reexamined: The Implications of the Quebra-Quilo Revolt, 1874–1875," *Hispanic American Historical Review* 57, 3 (August, 1977): 402–409.

p. 120. Quotations concerning the Cali disturbances come from J. León Helguera, "Antecedentes Sociales de la Revolución de 1851 en el Sur de Colombia (1848-1849)," *Anuario Colombiano de Historia Social y de la Cultura*, no. 5 (Bogotá, 1970), p. 55.

p. 121. E. J. Hobsbawm, *Primitive Rebels: Studies in Archaic Forms of Social Movement in the 19th and 20th Centuries* (New York: Norton, 1965).

pp. 122–123. The quotations from Tumpa can be found in Mario Gutierrez, *Sangre y Luz de Dos Razas* (La Paz, 1961), p. 89.

p. 124. The ideas of Tavares Bastos as well as the words of the President of the Province of Alagoas can be found in Carlos Pontes, *Tavares Bastos (Aureliano Cândido), 1839-1875* (São Paulo: Companhia Editora Nacional, 1939), pp. 54, 58.

p. 125. The poem on Antônio Silvino can be found in Manoel Calvalcanti Proença, ed., *Literatura Popular em Verso* (Rio de Janeiro: Casa de Rui Barbosa, 1964), I, 322-343. The quotation from *O Cearense* comes from Amaury de Souza, "The Cangaço and the Politic of Violence in Northeast Brazil," in Chilcote, *Protest and Resistance*, p. 120.

p. 125. Enrique López Albujar, *Los Caballeros del Delito. Estudio Criminológico del Bandolerismo en Algunos Departamentos del Peru* (Lima: Compañía de Impresiones y Publicidad, 1936), p. 40.

p. 126. Ignacio Manuel Altamirano, *El Zarco, the Bandit* (London: Folio Society, 1957), pp. 103-104, 58. The Guatemalan novella is by D. Bouquet y Soler, "Recuerdos de Copan-Calé," *El Noticioso* 1, 18 August, 2, 6, 23 September 1862.

pp. 128–129. Information in the following paragraphs is based on the current revisionists working in nineteenth-century Paraguayan history. I am particularly indebted to Richard Alan White, *Paraguay's Autonomous Revolution, 1810–1840* (Albuquerque: University of New Mexico Press, 1978); León Pomer, *La Guerra del Paraguay: Gran Negócio!* (Buenos Aires: Ediciones Caldén, 1968); Atilio Garciá Mellid, *Proceso a los Falsificadores de la Historia del Paraguay* (Buenos Aires: Ediciones Theoria, Vol. I, 1963; Vol. II, 1964); Carlos Pastore, *La Lucha por la Tierra en el Paraguay* (Montevideo: Editorial Antequera, 1972); Teresa Zárate, "Parcelación y Distribución de las Tierras Fiscales en el Paraguay (1870-1904)," *Revista Paraguaya de Sociología* Año 10, no. 26 (January-April 1973), pp. 121-140; Ezequiel González Alsina, "El Doctor Francia del Puebo," *Cuadernos Republicanos,* no. 8 (Asunción 1973), pp. 65-86; John Hoyt Williams, "Paraguay's 19th Century Estancias de La República," *Agricultural History* 47, 3 (July 1973): 206-216; Williams, "Foreign Técnicos and the Modernization of Paraguay, 1840-1870," *Journal of Interamerican Studies and World Affairs* 19, 2 (May 1977): 233-257; Thomas Lyle Whigham, "The Iron Works of Ibycui: Paraguayan Industrial Development in the Mid-Nineteenth Century," *The Americas* 35, 2 (October 1978): 201-218.

pp. 130–131. The quote from A. C. Tavares Bastos comes from his book *O Valle do Amazonas* (Rio de Janeiro: Garnier, 1866), p. 9. U.S. Minister to Brazil Henry T. Blow to Brazilian Foreign Minister Baron Cotegipe, April 1870, quoted in Norman T. Strauss, "Brazil after the Paraguayan War: Six Years of Conflict, 1870-7," *Journal of Latin American Studies* 10, 1 (May 1978): 23.

p. 131. Eliseo Reclus, *Paraguay* (Asunción: A. de Uribe, 1896), p. 87.

Chapter 7

pp. 133–134. Nathaniel H. Leff, "A Technique for Estimating Income Trends from Currency Data and an Application to Nineteenth-Century Brazil," *The Review of Income and Wealth,* 18th ser., no. 4 (December 1972), pp. 364-365. Charles C. Cumberland, *Mexico: The Struggle for Modernity* (New York: Oxford University Press, 1968), pp. 190-240. William Paul McGreevey, *An Economic History of Colombia, 1845-1930* (Cambridge: At the University Press, 1971), p. 146.

p. 134. The Mariátegui quotation comes from his *Seven Interpretive Essays,* p. 58. Also see pp. 68-69.

p. 136. John Coatsworth, "Railroads, Landholding, and Agrarian Protest in the Early Porfiriato," *Hispanic American Historical Review* 54, 1 (February 1974):70.

pp. 137-138. Kenneth V. Finney has made a valuable study of the New York and Honduras Rosario Mining Company. "Rosario and the Election of 1887: The Political Economy of Mining in Honduras," *Hispanic American Historical Review* 59, 1 (Feburary 1979): 81-107.

p. 139. The quotation from General Roca comes from Romero, *A History of Argentine Political Thought*, p. 193.

p. 140. The Justo quotation comes from the same source and page as above.

p. 140. Robin W. Winks, "On Decolonization and Informal Empire," *American Historical Review* 81, 3 (June 1976): 543.

p. 141. Graça Aranha, *Canaan* (Boston: The Four Seas Company, 1920), pp. 196-197.

p. 144. The statistic on the loss of communal lands in Mexico comes from Freidrich Katz, "Labor Conditions on Haciendas in Porfirian Mexico: Some Trends and Tendencies," *Hispanic American Historical Review* 54, 1(February 1974): 1. In an intriguing historical parallel, the Hawaiian monarch decreed the "Great Mehele," the land division of 1848, ending the chiefs' monopoly over the lands and making it possible for the common folk to acquire land. Alas, the Great Mehele only facilitated foreign acquisitions of Hawaiian land. "By the end of the nineteenth century white men owned four acres of land for every one owned by a native, and this included chiefs' lands." Gavan Daws, *Shoal of Time*, p. 128.

p. 145. On Panama see Walter LeFeber, *The Panama Canal: The Crisis in Historical Perspective* (New York: Oxford, 1978), p. 76. On Argentine food imports see Cortés Conde, *The First Stages of Modernization in Spanish America*, p. 19. On Mexican corn consumption see Eric Wolf, *Peasant Wars of the Twentieth Century* (New York: Harper & Row, 1969), p. 19.

p. 145. Charles H. Harris III, *A Mexican Family Empire: The Latifundio of the Sánchez Navarro Family, 1765-1867* (Austin: University of Texas Press, 1975).

pp. 145-146. Statistics on corn production are in Cumberland, *Mexico: The Struggle for Modernity*, p. 204; information on the fall of real wages is also in Cumberland, p. 232. The three newspaper quotations come from Meyer, *Problemas Campesinos*, pp. 222-223, 166.

p. 146. On the increased misery of the Indians under Díaz see Powell, "Mexican Intellectuals and the Indian Question," pp. 37-58; on the fall of real rural wages see Katz, "Labor Conditions on Haciendas in Porfirian Mexico," p. 1; on the declining diet of the rural worker see Cumberland, *Mexico: The Struggle for Modernity*, p. 204. Rodney D. Anderson indicates the "spectacular" rise of food prices at the turn of the century in Mexico. *Outcasts in Their Own Land: Mex-*

ican Industrial Workers, 1906–1911 (DeKalb: Northern Illinois University Press, 1976), p. 63.

pp. 146–147. Jonathan C. Brown presents evidence of the well-being of the gaucho in the first half of the nineteenth century in "Dynamic and Autonomy of a Traditional Marketing System; Buenos Aires, 1810–1860," *Hispanic American Historical Review* 56, 4 (November 1976): 605–629. On declining real wages see Aldo Ferrer, *The Argentinian Economy* (Berkeley and Los Angeles: University of California Pres,, 1967), p. 117, and Carl Solberg, "Farm Workers and the Myth of Export-Led Development in Argentina," *The Americas* 31, 2 (October 1974): 138. For specific information on the deteriorating condition of rural workers in Tucumán, including the quotations from *La Razón,* consult Manuel García Soriano, "La Condición Social del Trabajador en Tucumán durante el Siglo XIX," *Revisión Histórica* (Tucumán), año 1, no. 1 (May 1960), pp. 7–46. For Guatemala, there is the evidence presented by David J. McCreery, "Coffee and Class: The Structure of Development in Liberal Guatemala," *Hispanic American Historical Review* 56, 3 (August 1976): 438–460. Teresa Zárate indicates the deteriorating position of the Paraguayan peasant in "Parcelación de la Tierras," p. 133.

p. 147. For Chile, there are two studies by Arnold J. Bauer, "Chilean Rural Labor in the Nineteenth Century," *American Historical Review* 76, 4 (October 1971): 1059–1083; and *Chilean Rural Society from Spanish Conquest to 1930* (Cambridge: At the University Press, 1975). The quotation from Brian Loveman comes from *Chile: The Legacy of Hispanic Capitalism* (New York: Oxford, 1979), p. 163.

pp. 147–148. Nathaniel H. Leff, "Tropical Trade and Development in the Nineteenth Century: The Brazilian Experience," *Journal of Political Economy* 81, 3 (May-June 1973): 691. In another essay, Leff warns of the poor performance of the economy in the Northeast. "A Technique for Estimating Income Trends," p. 362. See also Freyre, *The Mansions and the Shanties,* p. 24. Peter L. Eisenberg, *The Sugar Industry in Pernambuco, 1840–1910: Modernization without Change* (Berkeley, Los Angeles, London: University of California Press, 1974), p. 214. At another point, Eisenberg affirmed, "The rural wage earners suffered a decreasing standard of living." (p. 189). Celso Furtado offered the same conclusion in *The Economic Growth of Brazil: A Survey from Colonial to Modern Times* (Berkeley and Los Angeles: University of California Press, 1963), p. 158. McGreevey, *An Economic History of Colombia,* p. 145. See also pp. 152, 154, 229.

p. 148. McGreevey's comments on the shift of urban income can be found in *An Economic History of Colombia,* p. 180. For declining industrial wages in Mexico, consult Cumberland, *Mexico, the Struggle* *for Modernity,* p. 224. Additional information on the plight of the Mexican urban working class can be found in Rodney D. Anderson, *Outcasts in Their Own land,* pp. 63-66.

pp. 148-149. James R. Scobie, *Buenos Aires: Plaza to Suburb (1870-1910)* (New York: Oxford University Press, 1974), pp. 137-140, 266, 268, 140-141. Ferrer, *The Argentine Economy,* p. 118.

p. 149. Eulália M. Lahmeyer Lobo, "Evolution des Prix et du Cout de la Vie a Rio de Janeiro (1820-1930)" in Colloques Internationaux du Centre Nacional de la Recherche Scientific, *L'Histoire Quantitative du Brésil de 1800 a 1930* (Paris, 1971), no. 543, pp. 211-212.

pp. 149-150. José A. Vandellos, *Ensayo de Demografía Venezolana* (Caracas: Ministerio de Fomento, 1938), p. 21. Information on Recife is based on figures presented by Bainbridge Cowell, Jr., "Cityward Migration and Population Structure: Recife, 1790-1920," a paper presented at the American Historical Association, San Francisco, December 28, 1978. Eduardo E. Arriago, *New Life Tables for Latin American Populations in the Nineteenth and Twentieth Centuries,* Population Monograph No. 3 (Berkeley: University of California, 1968), pp. 2-3. However, his nineteenth-century figures have been questioned by Nicolás Sánchez-Albornoz, *The Population of Latin America: A History* (Berkeley, Los Angeles, London: University of California Press, 1974), pp. 191-192. The life expectancy of 28.9 years comes from Sánchez-Abornoz, p. 192.

p. 153. The quote from Mariátegui can be found in John M. Baines, *Revolution in Peru: Mariátegui and the Myth* (University: University of Alabama Press, 1972), p. 83.

Population Growth by Nations

Argentina			Chile *(cont.)*		
1797	310,628	(1)	1865	1,819,223	(3)
1809	406,000	(1)	1875	2,075,971	(3)
1819	527,000	(1)	1885	2,507,005	(3)
1825	569,999	(1)	1895	2,695,625	(3)
1839	768,000	(1)	1900	2,904,000	(2)
1850	1,100,000	(2)	1907	3,231,022	(3)
1860	1,210,000	(1)	Colombia		
1869	1,737,976	(3)	1825	1,223,598	(3)
1895	3,954,911	(3)	1835	1,686,038	(3)
1900	4,743,000	(2)	1843	1,955,264	(3)
1914	7,885,347	(3)	1851	2,243,730	(3)
Bolivia			1864	2,694,487	(3)
1796	552,700	(4)	1870	2,391,984	(3)
1825	997,400	(4)	1900	3,825,000	(2)
1831	1,018,900	(3)	1905	4,143,632	(3)
1835	992,700	(3)	Costa Rica		
1845	1,031,500	(3)	1821	60,000	(6)
1850	1,374,000	(2)	1850	125,000	(2)
1854	1,544,300	(3)	1864	120,499	(3)
1882	1,097,600	(3)	1883	182,073	(3)
1900	1,696,400	(3)	1892	243,205	(3)
Brazil			1900	285,000	(2)
1798	2,288,000	(1)	Dominican Republic		
1819	3,596,000	(1)	1800	125,000	(7)
1830	5,340,000	(1)	1850	200,000	(2)
1850	7,205,000	(2)	1900	700,000	(2)
1860	8,418,000	(5)	Ecuador		
1872	10,112,061	(3)	1826	550,700	(8)
1880	11,748,000	(5)	1836	706,320	(8)
1890	14,333,915	(3)	1839	751,116	(8)
1900	17,318,556	(3)	1850	816,000	(2)
Chile			1900	1,400,000	(2)
1835	1,010,336	(3)	El Salvador		
1843	1,083,801	(3)	1821	270,000	(6)
1850	1,287,000	(2)	1850	394,000	(2)
1854	1,439,120	(3)	1900	932,000	(2)

Guatemala			Paraguay		
1821	510,000	(6)	1810	200,000	(9)
1850	850,000	(2)	1850	500,000	(2)
1880	1,224,602	(3)	1870	221,000	(10)
1893	1,364,678	(3)	1900	440,000	(2)
1900	1,425,000	(2)	Peru		
Haiti			1796	1,076,122	(11)
1788	455,000	(7)	1825	2,488,000	(11)
1850	938,000	(2)	1836	1,373,736	(3)
1900	1,270,000	(2)	1840	1,400,000	(1)
Honduras			1850	2,001,203	(3)
1801	130,000	(3)	1862	2,460,684	(3)
1821	150,000	(6)	1876	2,651,840	(3)
1850	350,000	(2)	1890	2,971,844	(1)
1881	307,289	(3)	1900	3,791,000	(1)
1887	331,917	(3)			
1900	443,000	(2)	Uruguay		
1910	553,446	(3)	1811	60,000	(12)
Mexico			1828	70,000	(12)
1803	5,764,731	(1)	1840	200,000	(12)
1810	6,122,354	(1)	1852	131,969	(3)
1824	6,500,000	(1)	1880	229,480	(3)
1830	7,996,000	(1)	1900	915,000	(2)
1842	7,015,509	(1)	1908	1,042,686	(3)
1850	7,662,000	(2)			
1857	8,247,660	(1)	Venezuela		
1870	9,100,000	(1)	1800	780,000	(13)
1880	9,000,000	(1)	1810	900,000	(13)
1895	12,632,427	(3)	1825	785,000	(13)
1900	13,607,259	(3)	1840	1,100,000	(13)
Nicaragua			1850	1,490,000	(2)
1821	180,000	(6)	1860	1,650,000	(13)
1850	300,000	(2)	1873	1,784,194	(3)
1867	257,000	(3)	1880	1,930,000	(13)
1900	448,000	(2)	1890	2,305,000	(13)
1906	505,377	(3)	1900	2,391,000	(13)

Sources:

(1) Richard E. Boyer and Keith A. Davies, *Urbanization in 19th Century Latin America: Statistics and Sources* (Los Angeles: UCLA Latin American Center, 1973).

(2) Nicolás Sánchez-Albornoz, *The Population of Latin America:A History* (Berkeley, Los Angeles, London: University of California Press, 1974).

(3) Kenneth Ruddle and Mukhtar Hamour, eds., *Statistical Abstract of Latin America 1969* (Los Angeles: UCLA Latin American Center, 1970).

(4) Astehio Averanga Mollinedo, *Aspectos Generales de la Población Boliviana* (La Paz: Libreria Editorial Juventud, 1974).

(5) Ministry of External Relations, *Brazil, 1966* (Rio de Janeiro, 1966).

(6) F. D. Parker, *The Central American Republics* (London: Oxford University Press, 1964).

(7) John E. Fagg, *Cuba, Haiti, and the Dominican Republic* (Englewood Cliffs, N.J.: Prentice-Hall, 1965).

(8) Manuel Villavicencio, *Geografía de la República del Ecuador* (New York: Craighead, 1858).

(9) Mary W. Williams, *The People and Politics of Latin America* (New York: Ginn & Co., 1930).

(10) Omar Díaz de Arce, *Paraguay* (Havana: Casa de las Americs, 1967).

(11) Henry E. Dobyns and Paul L. Doughty, *Peru: A Cultural History* (New York: Oxford University Press, 1976).

(12) Russell H. Fitzgibbon, *Uruguay: Portrait of a Democracy* (London: George Allen & Unwin, 1956).

(13) José A. Vandellos, *Ensayo de Demografía Venezolana* (Caracas: Ministerio de Fomento, 1936).

Urban Population Statistics

I. Percentage of National Populations Living in Cities of More Than 10,000 Inhabitants, Circa 1900.[1]

Argentina	27.1
Bolivia	8.0
Brazil	10.9
Chile	21.8
Colombia	9.4
Costa Rica	28.4
Cuba	30.7
Ecuador	12.3
El Salvador	15.4
Guatemala	16.9
Honduras	8.4
Mexico	12.7
Paraguay	16.5
Peru	7.4
Uruguay	30.0
Venezuela	22.8

II. Population Growth of Selected Major Latin American Cities throughout the Nineteenth Century.

Bogota, Colombia[2]	
1825	40,000
1843	40,000
1851	40,000
1870	41,000
1884	96,000
1893	120,000
1905	100,000

Buenos Aires, Argentina[3]	
1801	40,000
1810	44,800
1822	55,416
1836	64,126
1855	90,076
1865	150,000
1870	186,320

Buenos Aires *(cont.)*

1875	230,000
1887	433,375
1895	663,854
1914	1,575,814

Caracas, Venezuela[4]

1800	31,000
1810	42,000
1816	21,000
1839	35,000
1847	34,000
1857	44,000
1873	49,000
1881	56,000
1891	72,000
1920	92,000

Córdoba, Argentina[5]

1801	11,500
1825	10,000
1839	14,187
1855	15,000
1869	28,523
1895	47,609
1914	104,894

Guadalajara, Mexico[6]

1803	19,500
1813	50,000
1827	60,000
1852	63,000
1874	75,000
1885	80,000
1895	83,870
1900	101,208

Lima, Peru[7]

1791	52,627
1812	63,900
1820	64,628
1836	54,628
1844	60,000
1856	94,195
1862	89,434
1876	100,488
1891	103,956
1903	139,289

Mexico City, Mexico[8]

1803	137,000
1811	168,846
1820	179,830
1838	205,430
1852	170,000
1862	200,000
1870	200,000
1880	250,000
1895	329,274
1900	344,721

Puebla, Mexico[9]

1803	67,800
1820	60,000
1852	71,631
1862	72,817
1882	72,817
1895	91,917
1900	93,521

Rio de Janeiro, Brazil[10]

1799	43,376
1807	50,000
1815	100,000
1821	112,695
1838	137,078
1849	266,466
1856	181,158
1870	235,381
1890	522,651
1895	650,000
1906	811,433

Rosario, Argentina[11]

1801	400
1815	763
1842	1,500
1858	9,785
1887	50,914
1895	92,717
1900	112,461
1914	226,214

Salvador, Brazil[12]

1800	100,000
1809	100,000
1819	100,000

Salvador *(cont.)*		Santiago *(cont.)*	
1835	130,000	1895	256,000
1852	150,000	1907	333,000
1872	129,109	São Paulo, Brazil[14]	
1890	173,879	1790	8,000
1900	205,813	1820	20,000
Santiago, Chile[13]		1836	12,256
1800	30,000	1855	15,471
1813	35,000	1872	23,243
1835	70,000	1886	44,030
1865	115,000	1890	64,934
1875	130,000	1893	129,409
1885	189,000	1900	239,820

1. Nicolás Sánchez-Albornoz, *The Population of Latin America: A History* (Berkeley, Los Angeles, London: University of California Press, 1974), pp. 178-179.

2. Edward Friedel and Michael F. Jimenez, "Colombia," in Richard M. Morse, ed., *The Urban Development of Latin America* (Stanford, Calif.: Stanford University Center for Latin American Studies, 1971), p. 62.

3. Richard E. Boyer and Keith A. Davies, *Urbanization in 19th-Century Latin America: Statistics and Sources* (Los Angeles: UCLA Latin American Center, 1973), p. 7.

4. John Galey, "Venezuela," in Morse, *The Urban Development*, p. 111.

5. Boyer and Davies, *Urbanization*, p. 9.

6. Ibid., p. 37.

7. Ibid., pp. 59-60.

8. Ibid., pp. 41-42.

9. Ibid., p. 47.

10. Ibid., p. 23.

11. Ibid., p. 11.

12. Ibid., p. 25.

13. Michael L. Conniff, "Chile," in Morse, *The Urban Development*, p. 54.

14. Boyer and Davies, *Urbanization*, p. 28.

GLOSSARY

Cacique An Indian chief; it has also come to mean a local political boss

Caudillo A strong leader who wields complete power over his subordinates

Compardio A godparent relationship

Conventillo Tenement house

Corrido Ballad

Costumbrismo A literary genre that emphasizes local customs and manners

Criollo In Argentina, this term refers to one born in the New World, a locally born Argentine as contrasted with an immigrant

Curandero A practitioner of folk medicine

Ejído The common land held by Indian communities and used for agriculture in Mexico

Gaucho The cowboy of the Pampas

Guaso Chilean cowboy or person of the countryside

Hacendados The owner of a large estate in Spanish America; the comparable term for Brazil is *fazendeiro*

Inquilinaje The system of rural tenancy in Chile

Inquilino A tenant farmer in Chile

Latifundio, latifundia Large estates

Latifundista The owner of a large estate in Latin America

Llanero A cowboy of the southern plains of Venezuela

Mandamientos A system of forced Indian labor

Mestizo A person of mixed parentage; usually it refers to a European-Indian mixture

Moneda nacional National currency

Mulatto A person of mixed parentage; usually it refers to a European-African mixture

Pampas The extensive plains and prairies of Argentina and Uruguay

Payador A popular minstrel

Pueblo The people

Vil população Portuguese for "vile population," meaning the lower classes

INDEX

Abreu, João Capistrano de, 36, 70

Acosta, Cecilio, 36

Adalbert, Prince, 115-116

Africans, 89; in New World considered as obstacles to progress, 29-30; contributions to New World, 43

Agrarian reform. See Land reform

Agriculture, 134 ff.

Alamán, Lucas, 38, 40, 41, 44-45

Alberdi, Juan Bautista, 51, 54-56; critical of Generation of 1837, 52-53; on caudillos, 91 ff.

Albornaz P., Oswaldo, 113

Albujar, Enrique López, 125

Alencar, José de, 64

Altamirano, Ignacio Manuel, 81 ff., 126

Alternatives to Europeanization, 86 ff.

Amalia, 24

Aramayo, Félix Avelino, 22

Aramayo, José Avelino, 20

Arana, Diego Barros, 38, 41, 46

Aranha, J. P. de Graça, 140-141

Araucanian Indians, 114

Argentina, 14, 32-33, 49, 57, 60-62, 93, 94, 109, 114, 129-130, 135, 137, 145, 146, 151-152; ideology of progress in, 21 ff.; folk alternatives in, 88

ff.; popular protest in, 120-121; millenarian movements, 123; differing views of foreign investment in, 139-140; declining quality of life for masses in, 147 ff.

Arriago, Eduardo E., 150

Artigas, José G., 67, 92

Atusparia, Pedro Pablo, 114

Avellaneda, Gerturdis Gómez de, 116-117

Aves Sin Nido, 25 ff.

Azevedo; Aluizio, 117

Bahia, 115, 117

Balaiada, 118

Balmes, Miguel Boada y, 102

Banderas, Juan, 110

Banditry, 118, 121, 125-127; in literature, 126-127

Barbarism, 22, 119; the concept denoting traditional and backwardness to the elites, 18; struggle between civilization and, 21 ff., 125; perceived as a threat by the elites, 23-24, 112; questioning of barbarity-civilization dichotomy, 53 ff.

Barbosa, Januário da Cunha, 40, 41

Barrios, Justo Rufino, 46, 105, 106

Barros, Alvaro Gabriel, 57

Bastos, A. C. Tavares, 124, 131

Batlle, José, 80, 92

Designer: Graphics Two
Compositor: Freedmen's Organization
Printer: Braun-Brumfield, Inc.
Binder: Braun-Brumfield, Inc.
Text: Compuwriter IV Baskerville
Display: Compuwriter IV Baskerville
Cloth: Joanna Oxford 32300
Paper: 50 lb P&S Vellum, acid-free